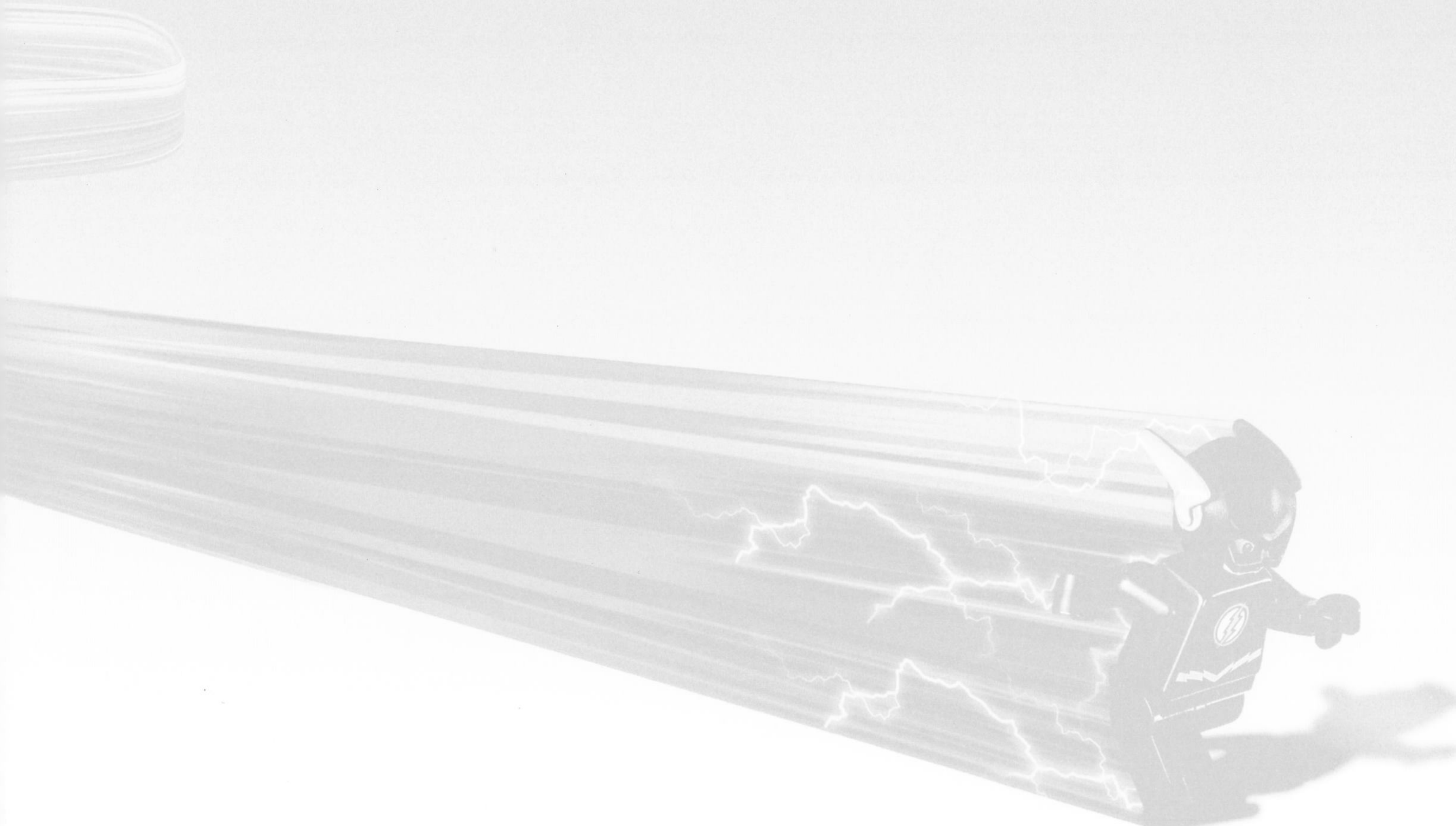

LEGO® DC COMICS SUPER HEROES

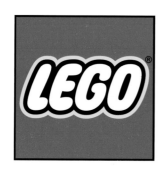

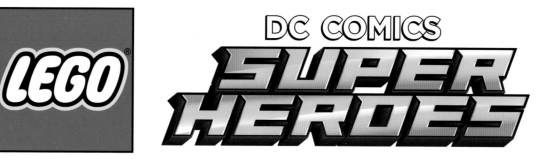

THE AWESOME GUIDE

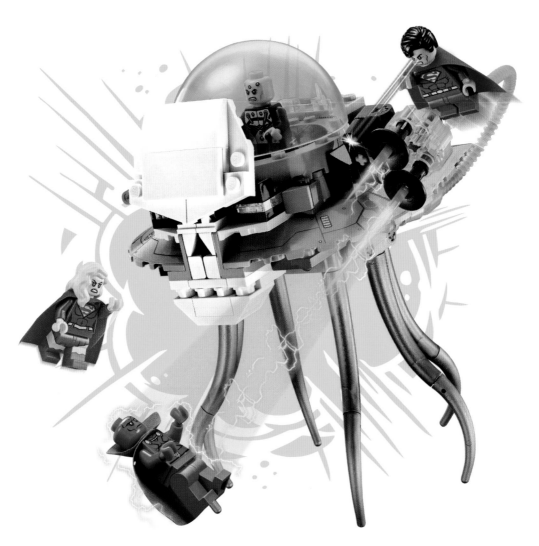

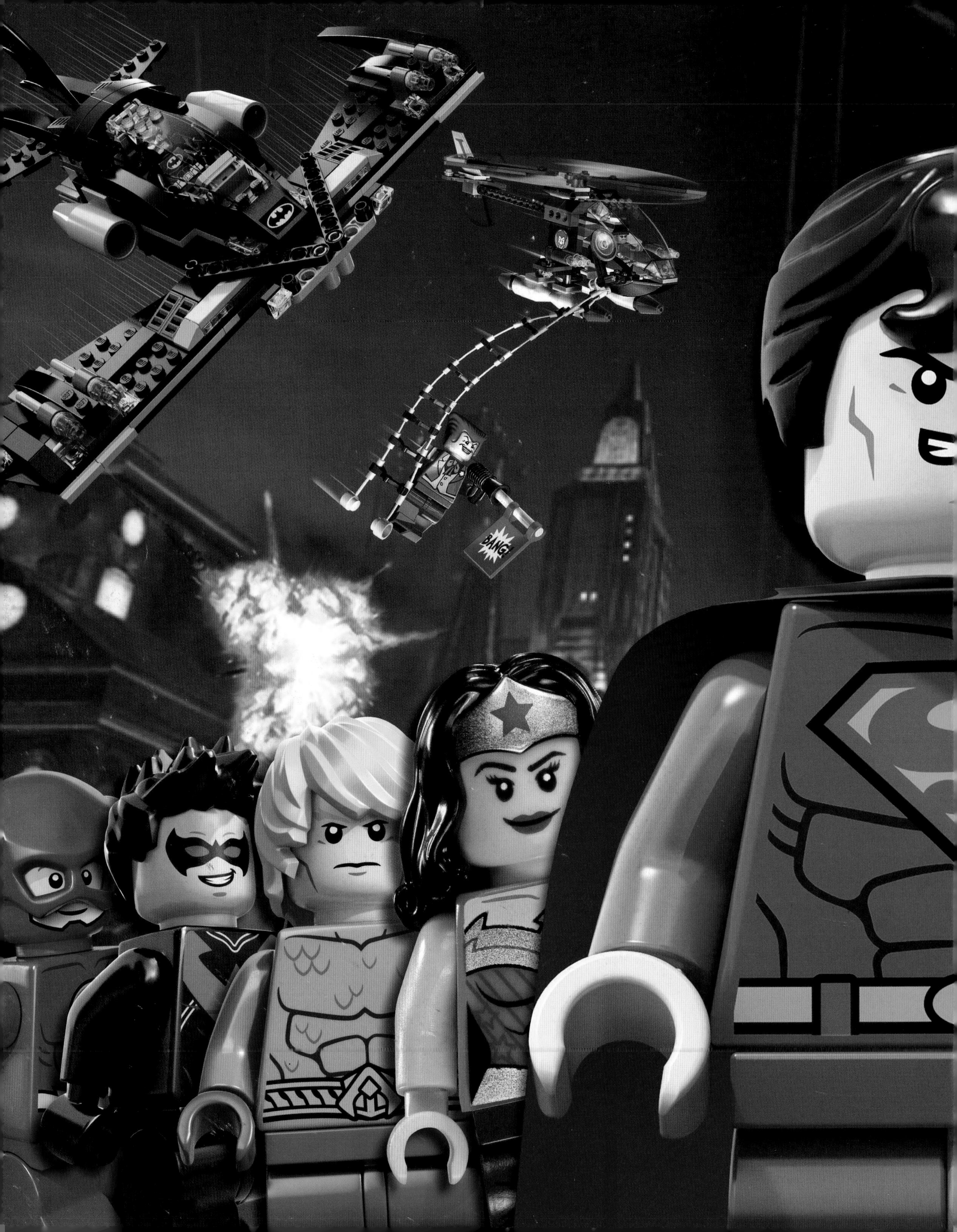
BANG!

DC COMICS

LEGO SUPER HEROES

THE AWESOME GUIDE

written by Cavan Scott

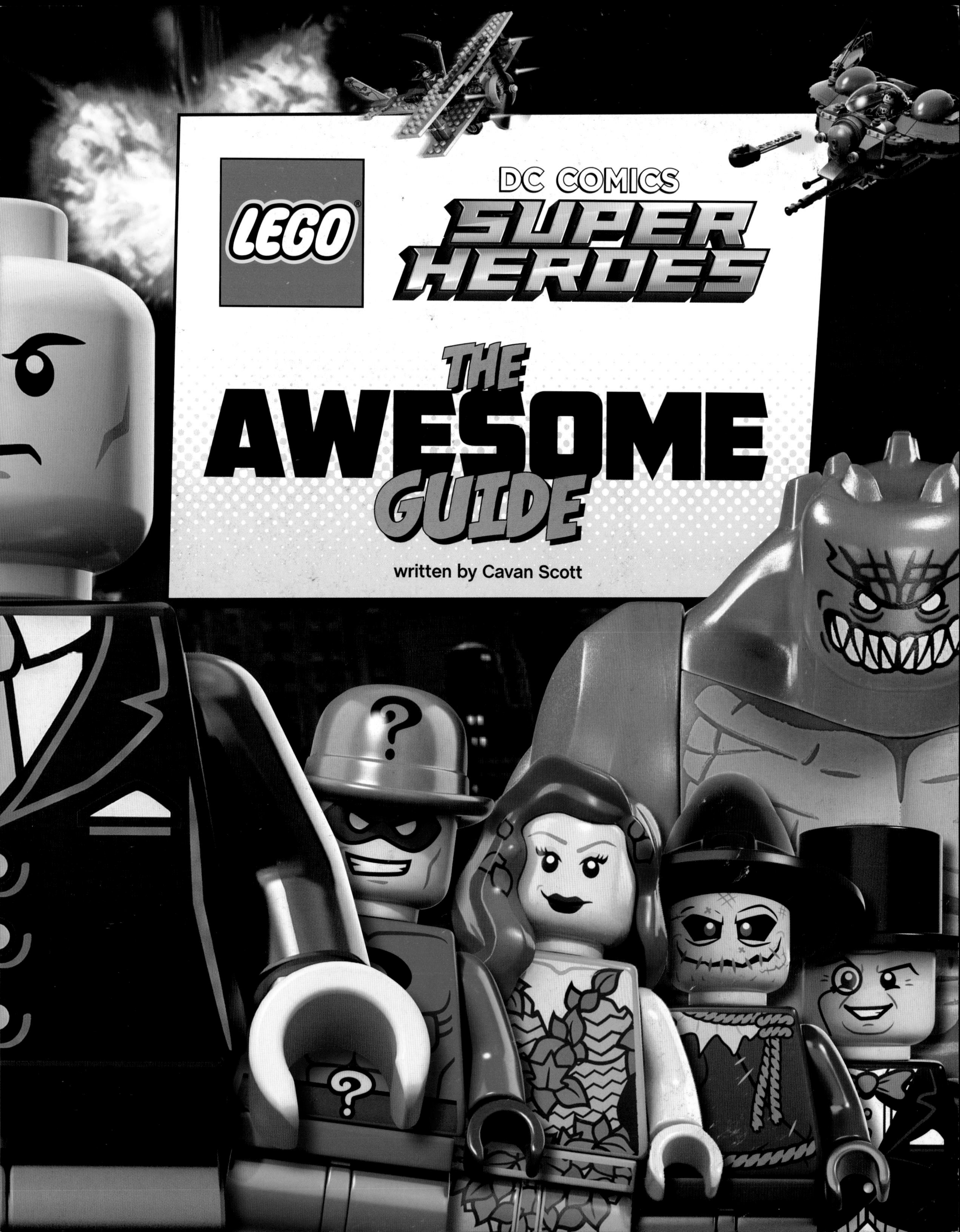

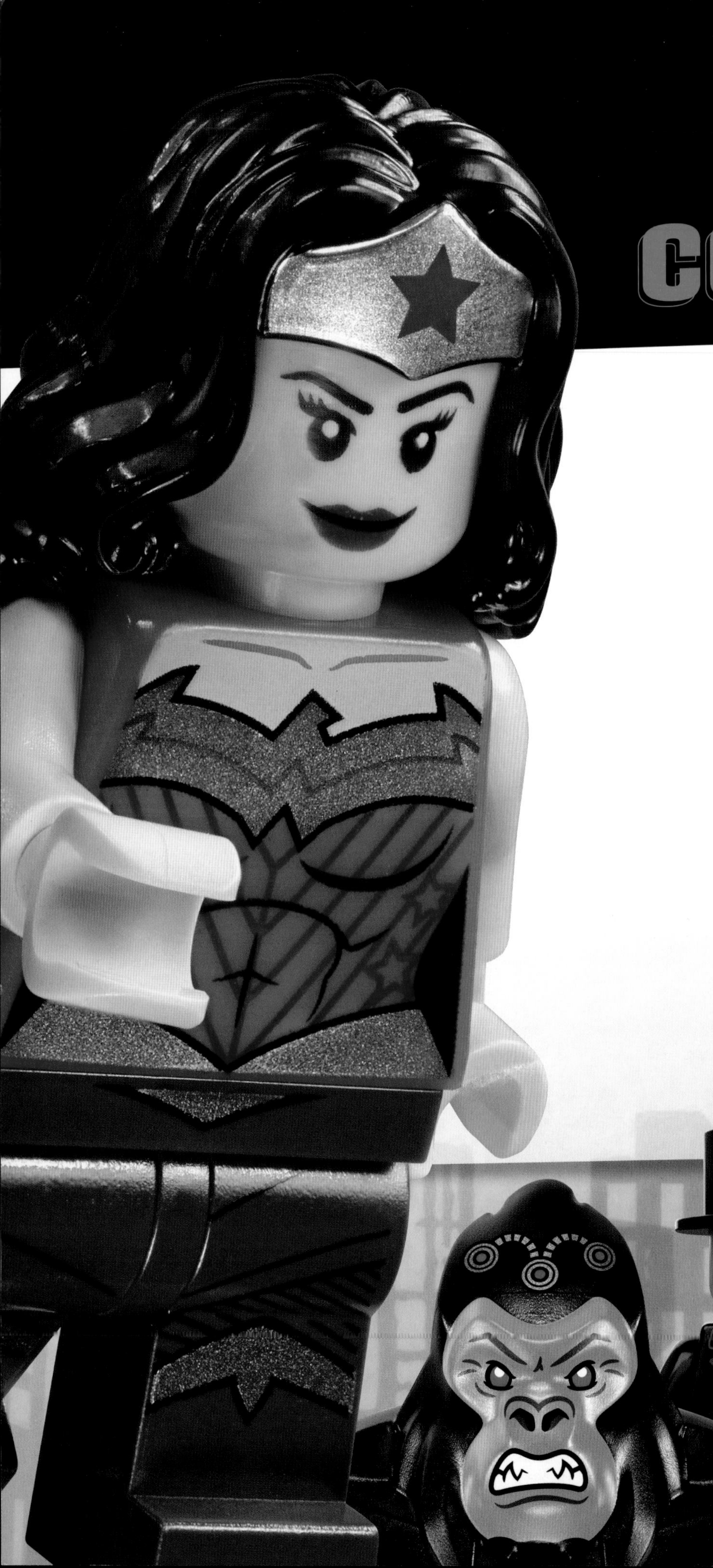

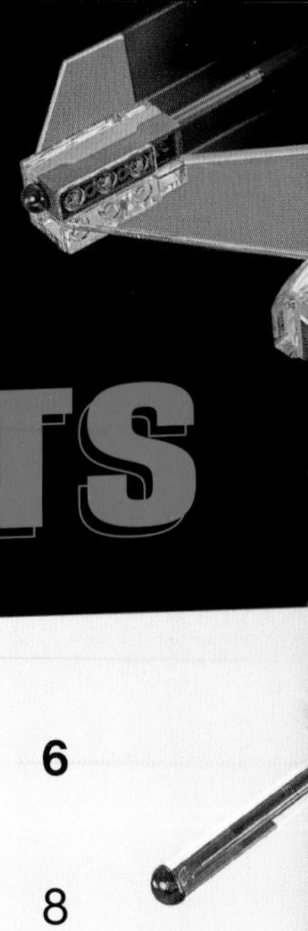

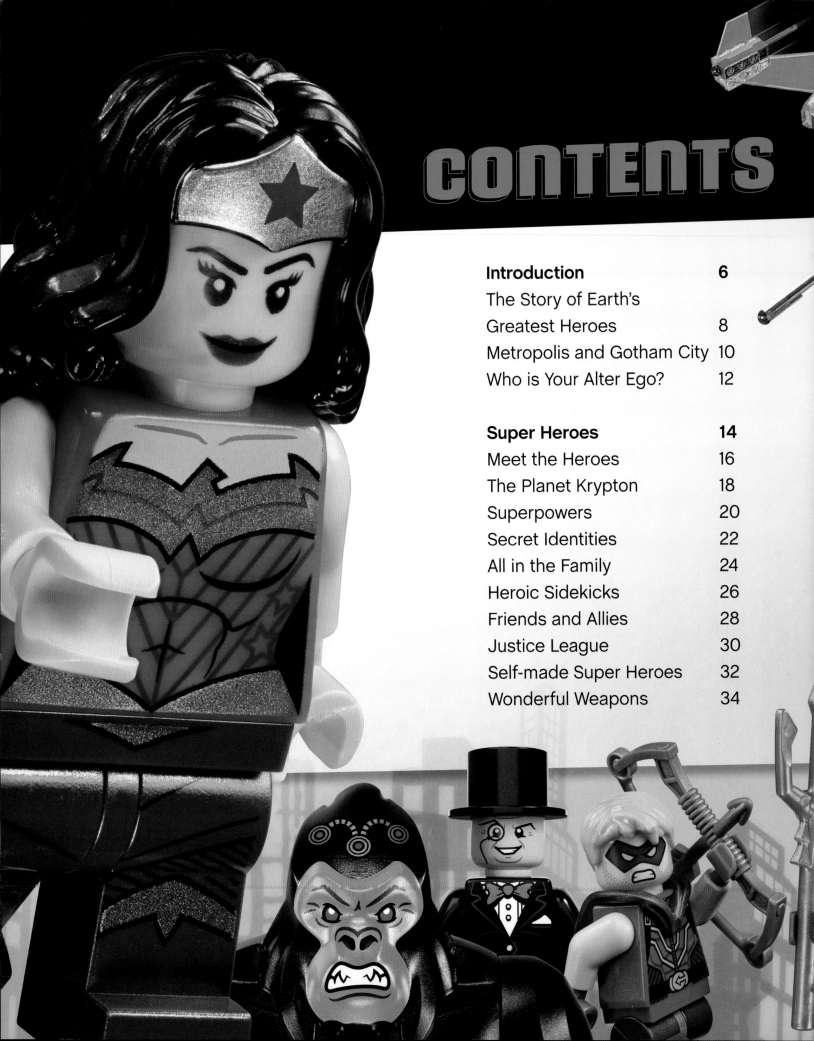

CONTENTS

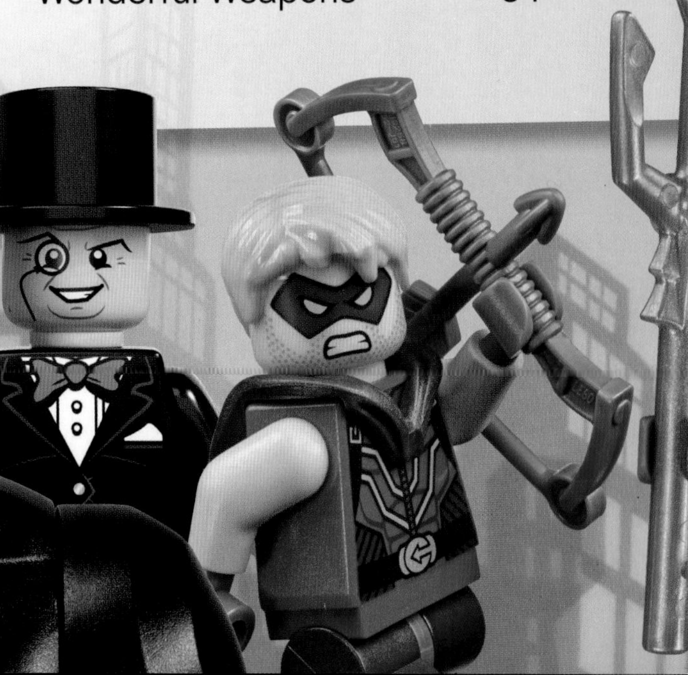

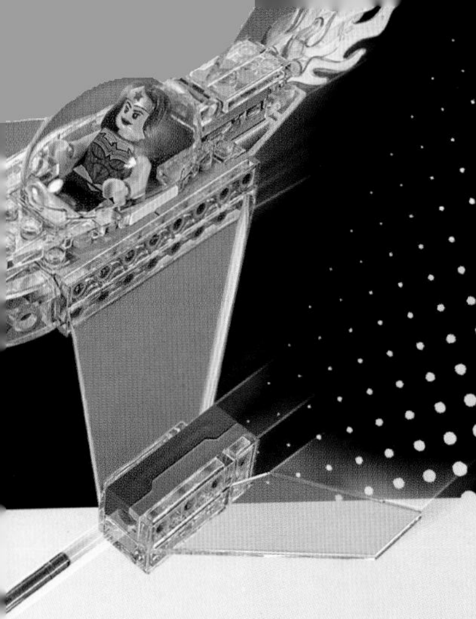

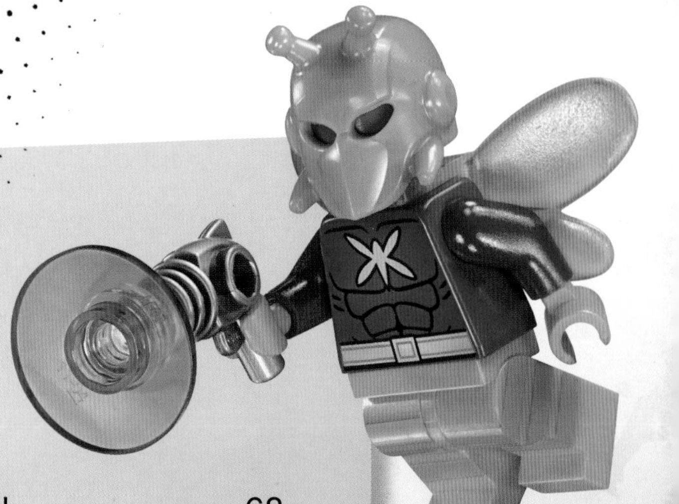

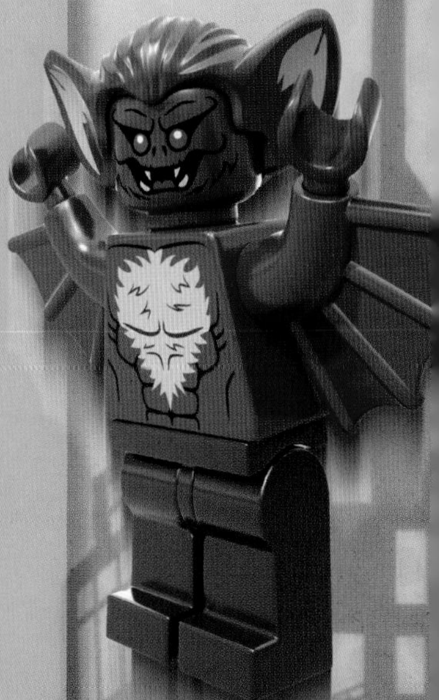

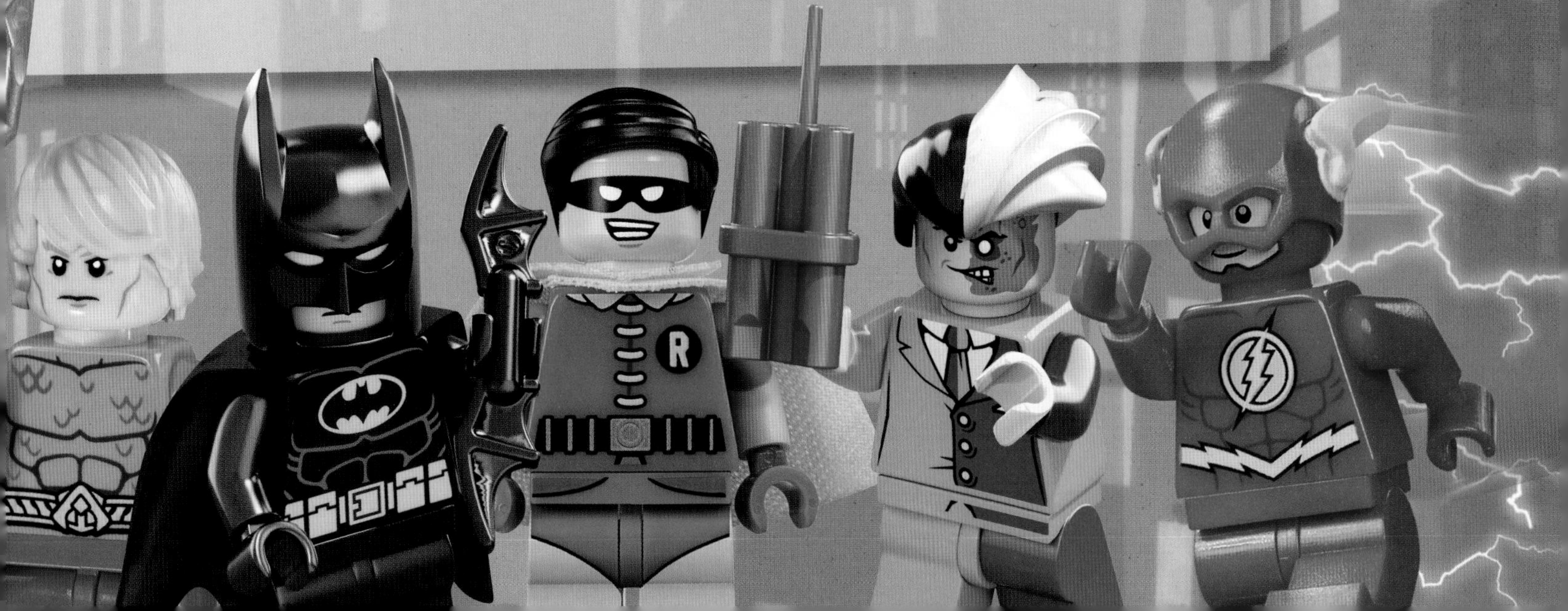

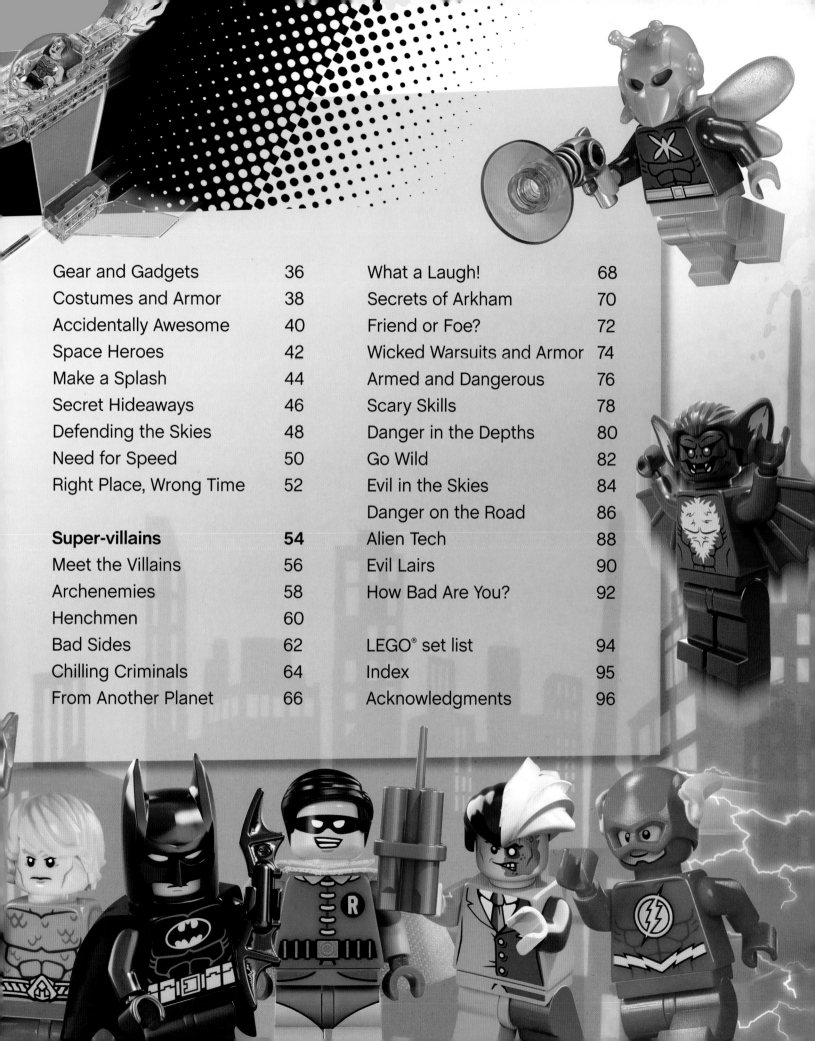

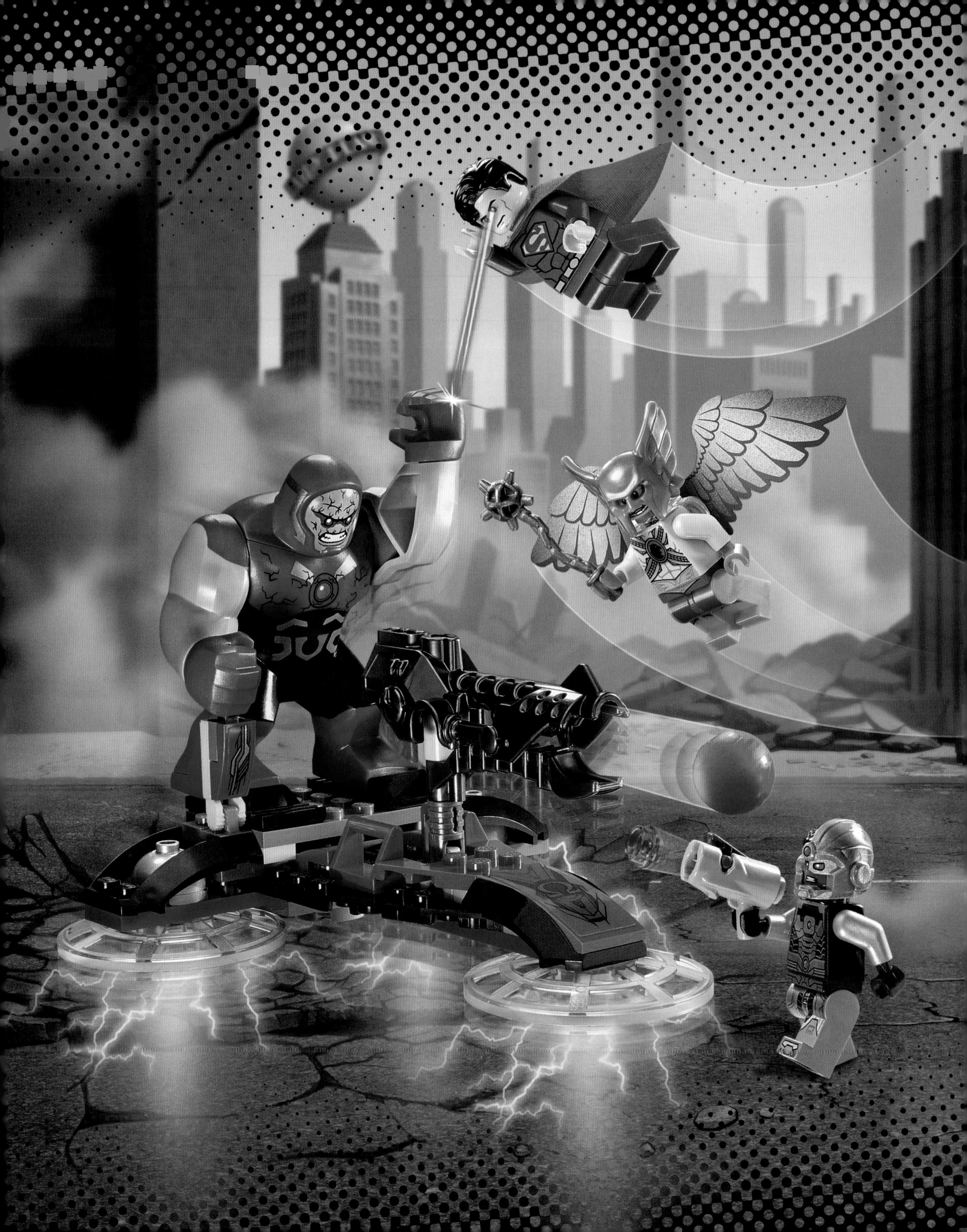

INTRODUCTION

Ever wondered where Superman got his powers, or how The Flash became so speedy? Or why Wonder Woman flies an Invisible Jet, and why Batman has so many cool vehicles? All the answers and more can be found in this totally awesome guide to LEGO® DC Comics Super Heroes.

Discover the origins of the Justice League and their secret identities. Gasp at their amazing superpowers and learn all about their incredible collections of gadgets and vehicles.

Boo the long line of super-villains and their horrible henchmen. Find out about their wicked weapons and uncover their evil schemes to A) take over the Earth and B) take over the Earth. That's mainly what super-villains are into, after all. That, and stealing lots of money, turning everyone into giggling zombies, or shrinking the Earth until it's small enough to fit in a jar...

Thankfully, the Super Heroes are always ready to unite and stop the super-villains' fiendish plans.

Who will win the fight between good and evil?

It's time to find out!

THE STORY OF EARTH'S GREATEST HEROES

SUPERMAN, BATMAN, WONDER WOMAN, and co. lead the way in the fight against evil. Discover how the Justice League and other awesome Super Hero teams work together against the forces of darkness.

SHE'S A WONDER

Far away, warrior princess Diana lives on a tropical island populated only by women. Everything changes when a plane crash-lands in the middle of her paradise home. Saving the pilot's life, Diana realizes that there is a world she never knew existed. She takes to the skies as the Super Hero, Wonder Woman.

STRANGE VISITOR FROM ANOTHER PLANET

With the arrival of Superman, the world becomes aware of Super Heroes. His first public act is to save a plane from crashing into the center of Metropolis. The people of the world gasp. Here is a man who can fly, who can lift unbelievable weights, and who can travel at incredible speeds! Planet Earth will never be the same again.

GOTHAM CITY'S GUARDIAN

Meanwhile, Gotham City is being protected by a mysterious masked vigilante. Most people believe that Batman is nothing more than an urban legend, until the crazy crimes of the Joker bring the Dark Knight out of the shadows.

DYNAMIC DUO

At first, Batman works alone, but in time he takes on an apprentice. Robin, the Boy Wonder, joins the Dark Knight's fight against crime. By day, they are billionaire Bruce Wayne and his young ward, Dick Grayson. By night, they are the Dynamic Duo, bringing justice to Gotham's streets.

JOINING FORCES

New Super Heroes arrive on the scene, including The Flash, Aquaman, and Green Lantern. Together with Superman and Wonder Woman, they form a new Super Hero team, the Justice League, and invite Batman to join them.

HEROES UNITED

Batman isn't sure he wants to be part of a team. But with terrifying intergalactic villains threatening Earth, Batman learns that the Justice League is stronger together. Now, based in the impressive Hall of Justice in Metropolis, the League protects the world from evil.

BRING ON THE BAD GUYS

There is no time to rest for the Justice League. With every new hero comes a host of vile villains, ready to take over the world. Often led by criminal mastermind Lex Luthor, these bothersome bad guys regularly join forces to bring down the Justice League.

ALIEN ATTACK

Even the skies aren't safe. Alien villains, like the warlord Darkseid, turn their attention to Earth, wanting to conquer the planet.

TITANIC TEAM-UP

But Earth is protected. Robin leaves Batman's side to become Nightwing, founding the Teen Titans alongside Cyborg, Starfire, and Beast Boy. The young heroes stand shoulder to shoulder with the Justice League against the villains of the universe.

FUTURE HEROES

Batman discovers the existence of a new generation of champions, the Legion of Super-Heroes, who protect Metropolis in the future. The fight goes on. Who will win the battle between good and evil? Only time will tell...

METROPOLIS

Two cities dominate the world of DC Comics Super Heroes—and they couldn't be more different! Metropolis is a gleaming futuristic city, protected by Superman, while Gotham City is a gloomy place of crime and villainy. No wonder it needs a hero like Batman!

LEXCORP

Believe it or not, most citizens of Metropolis believe that villainous Lex Luthor is a good guy! The LexCorp tower is one of the most recognizable landmarks in the city—mainly because vain Lex deliberately built it to be the tallest tower in the city.

HALL OF JUSTICE

The headquarters of the Justice League, where the League trains and relaxes, stands in the heart of Metropolis. The Hall's central computer is linked to numerous satellites that constantly monitor the Earth for super-villain activity.

STAT SCAN

NAME:	Metropolis
ALSO KNOWN AS:	The Big Apricot
FOUNDED:	1634
POPULATION:	11 million
BEST KNOWN FOR:	Innovation and business
PLACES TO VISIT:	The Superman Museum, The Superman Memorial Statue

UNIVERSE IN UNITS

1775

The year the *Daily Planet* was first published!

THE *DAILY PLANET*

The *Daily Planet* building stands tall on the Metropolis skyline. Here, reporters Clark Kent and Lois Lane compete to impress editor Perry White. Lex Luthor once tried to steal the globe that spins at the top of the tower, but his plan backfired when the ornamental planet landed on top of him. Whoops!

GOTHAM CITY

WAYNE TOWER

This skyscraper is the headquarters of Wayne Enterprises, Bruce Wayne's multi-billion-dollar company. The building is a sign of hope for citizens of Gotham City, showing that you can reach for the skies even in a city as corrupt as Gotham.

WAYNE MANOR

Not all places in Gotham are sinister or spooky. The stately Wayne Manor is found on the outskirts of the city and is the ancestral home of Bruce Wayne.

STAT SCAN

NAME:	Gotham
ALSO KNOWN AS:	The worst place to vacation... ever!
FOUNDED:	1635
POPULATION:	10 million
BEST KNOWN FOR:	Being home to the worst bad guys in the history of villainy
PLACES TO AVOID:	Arkham Asylum, Blackgate Penitentiary, Crime Alley

INFO BLAST

OUT OF THIS WORLD

Not all heroes are from Earth. Hawkman comes from the highly advanced planet Thanagar. His gravity-defying armor is made from special Thanagarian metal. Martian Manhunter is the last survivor of Mars, and Superman escaped from his home planet, Krypton, just before it was destroyed.

"I'M NOT PARTICULARLY FOND OF GOTHAM. IT'S LIKE SOMEONE BUILT A NIGHTMARE OUT OF METAL AND STONE!"

WHO IS YOUR ALTER EGO?

Ever wondered who you might be if you lived in the same world as the Justice League heroes and their wicked archenemies? Discover if you are a hero, friend, ordinary bystander, or, gulp, villain!

Would you like to have superpowers, or skills you learn yourself?

SKILLS I LEARN MYSELF

SUPERPOWERS

TO TAKE OVER THE WORLD

Why do you want superpowers?

Do you want to fight crime?

TO HELP PEOPLE

YES

Are you ready to train your body and mind to the peak of perfection?

NO

Would you want to commit crime?

YES

YES

NO

NO

You're a Super Hero like Batman. You may not have powers, but you push yourself to the limit to save your city.

You're a good friend to the Super Heroes, like Commissioner Gordon. Just because you're not in the Justice League, it doesn't mean you're not a hero!

You're an everyday citizen, but that doesn't mean you're not special. Just watch out for those super-villains!

Oh no! You're a super-villain like Gorilla Grodd. You use your powers for evil.

You're an awesome Super Hero from another planet, like Supergirl, who now protects Earth.

Do you ever wish you came from outer space?

YES

NO

Would you get your superpowers by accident?

You're a legendary Super Hero, like Wonder Woman, who has always had superpowers.

YES

NO, I WOULD BE BORN WITH THEM

Do you always have to be in charge?

YES

NO

You're a cunning criminal mastermind like the Penguin.

Grrr. You're a horrible henchman, always following the orders of your criminal boss!

Wow! How lucky are you? A twist of fate has turned you from ordinary human to Super Hero, like The Flash.

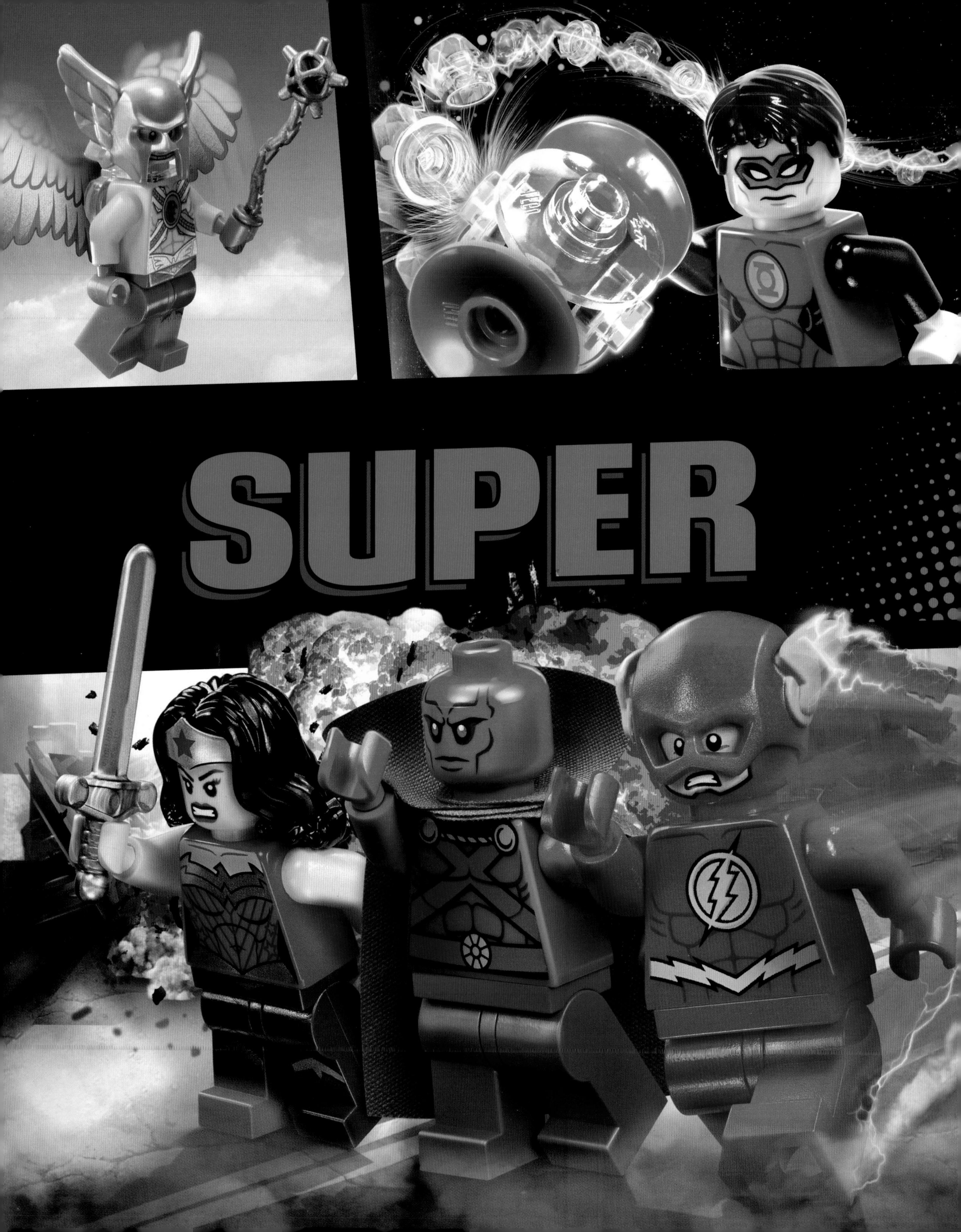
SUPER

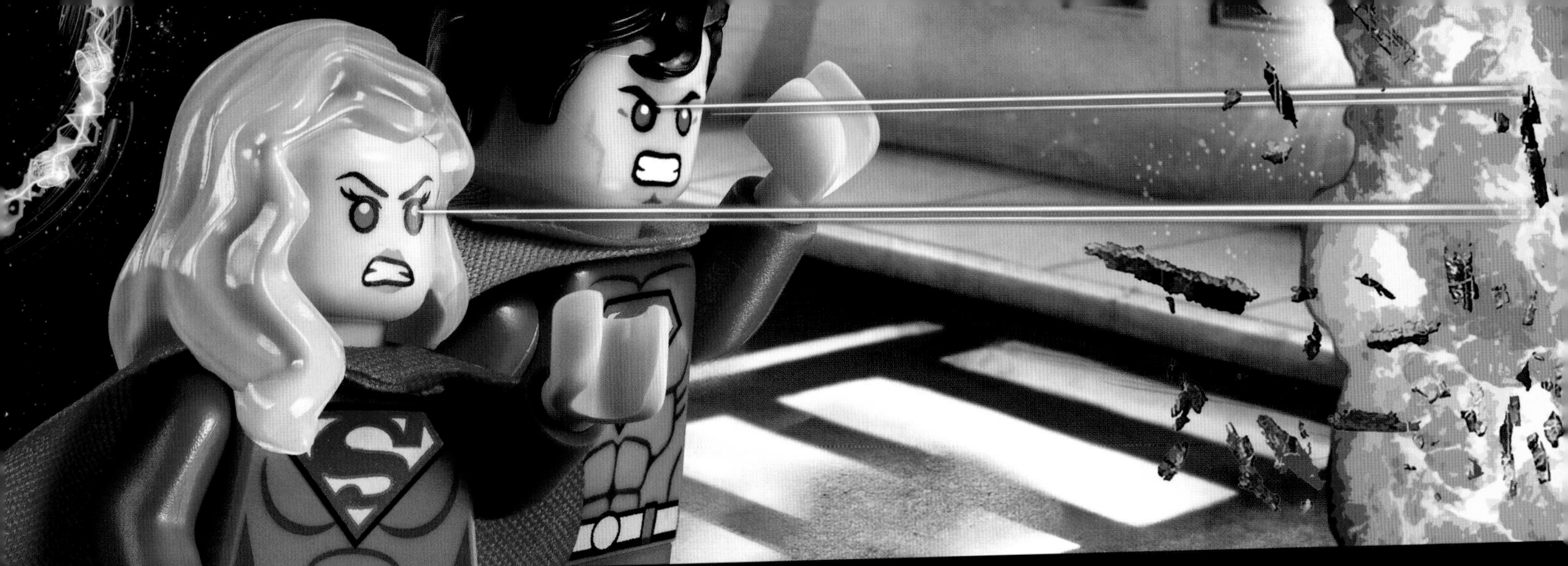

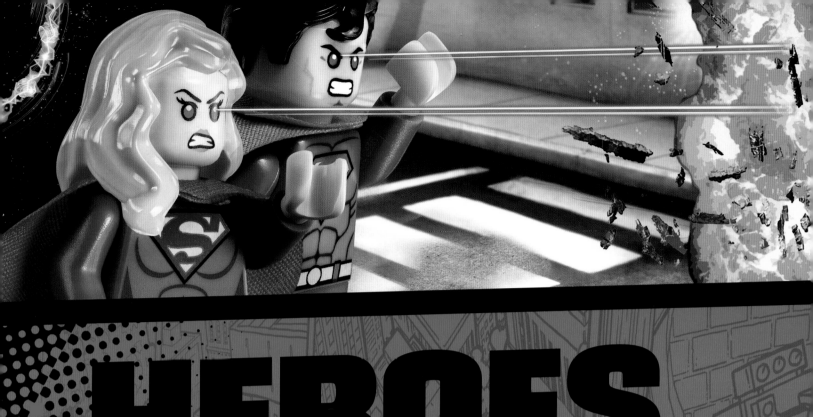

HEROES

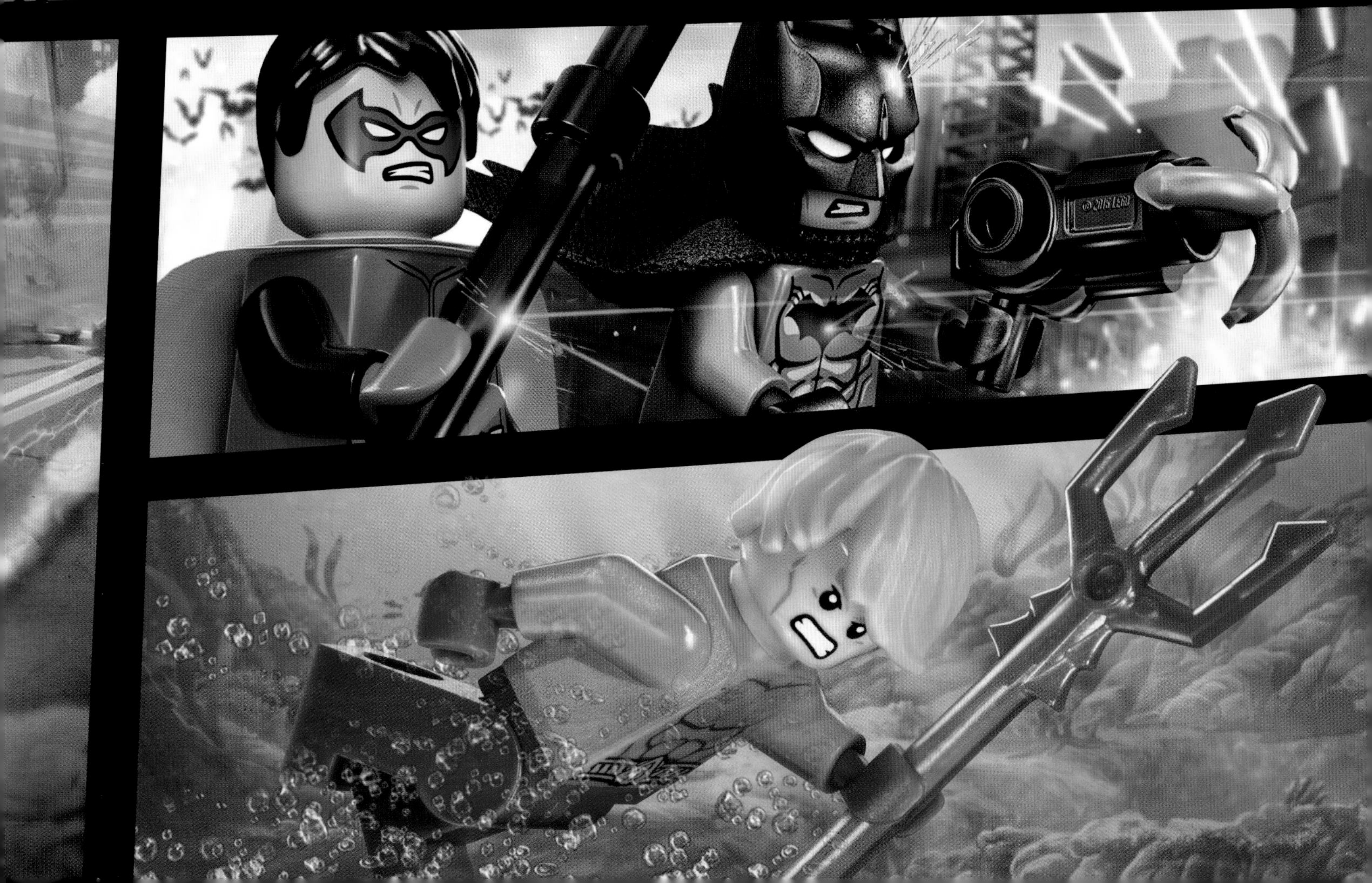

MEET THE HEROES

Whether they're rescuing kittens from trees or stopping the destruction of Earth, this band of heroes never rests. Brave, courageous, and dressed to impress, LEGO® DC Comics Super Heroes are the best of the best.

GREEN ARROW
An awesome archer, Green Arrow is able to hit any target with his arrows.

AQUAMAN
As King of Atlantis, this underwater Super Hero is the sworn defender of the seas.

LIGHTNING LAD
This hero from the future can generate electricity from his bare hands.

MARTIAN MANHUNTER
The last survivor of the Red Planet, this alien is able to disguise himself as any man or woman.

SUPERBOY
Villain Lex Luthor created this clone of Superman, but he now sides with the good guys.

ROBIN
Also known as the Boy Wonder, this young hero is Batman's prank-loving sidekick.

ARSENAL
Green Arrow's speedy sidekick is a great shot with his longbow.

WONDER WOMAN
This Amazon warrior princess now fights to protect the Earth.

BATMAN
The Dark Knight is the tireless protector of Gotham City. He likes black—a lot.

SUPERMAN
A strange visitor from another planet, Superman is the ultimate good guy.

CYBORG
Half-man, half-machine, Cyborg is the newest member of the Justice League.

HAWKMAN
In his lighter-than-air armor, this flying Super Hero brings justice from the skies.

BLUE BEETLE
Blue Beetle is armored from head to toe thanks to a mysterious alien scarab beetle.

KATANA
Mistress of the martial arts, Katana wields magic swords ready to slice and dice enemies.

BEAST BOY
This Teen Titan is able to take the form of any animal on Earth.

PLASTIC MAN
The stretchiest hero alive, Plastic Man can contort his body into all kinds of shapes.

COSMIC BOY
Hailing from the planet Braal, Cosmic Boy can create powerful magnetic fields.

THE ATOM
With his ability to shrink down to microscopic proportions, Atom shows that heroes come in all shapes and sizes!

THE FLASH
The Flash is the Fastest Man Alive. The speedy hero is fast-talking, too!

NIGHTWING
Trained by Batman, this former Robin now wages his own war against crime.

SHAZAM
The World's Mightiest Mortal, Shazam was given his magical powers by a wizard.

STARFIRE
This alien teen is able to harness the power of the stars themselves.

GREEN LANTERN
This hero defends Earth using the power of his emerald alien ring.

SUPERGIRL
Also known as the Girl of Steel, Supergirl possesses all of Superman's powers—and some more of her own.

BATGIRL
The police commissioner's daughter is now a brave crime fighter in her own right.

STRANGE

Kryptonian mythology influenced Dick Grayson's choice of Super Hero name. He chose Nightwing, which is also the name of a legendary Kryptonian dragon.

This set was exclusive to San Diego Comic-Con 2015. It references the scene on the cover of the very first Superman comic, *Action Comics* #1

AWESOME!

Superman may be known as Clark Kent on Earth, but on Krypton he was given the name Kal-El.

HEROES IN NUMBERS

145 bricks

Included in the Action Comics #1 Superman (set SDCC2015-3), which pays homage to the cover of the first Superman comic

27.1 light years

The distance between Krypton and Earth

4 moons

Krypton's moons were called Wegthorn, Koron, Mithen, and Xenon

1 set

Features Superman's fellow Kryptonian, Supergirl—Brainiac Attack (set 76040).

BRICK-SIZED FACT

Reverse the head of most Kryptonian minifigures to reveal glowing red heat-vision eyes!

Lifting a car is problem for Kryptonians like Superman

STAT SCAN

NAME:	Superman
OTHER NAMES:	Clark Kent, Kal-El
FRIENDS:	Lois Lane, Jimmy Olsen
FOES:	Lex Luthor
LIKES:	Truth, justice, and fair play
DISLIKES:	Lies and injustice

THE PLANET KRYPTON

UNIVERSE IN UNITS

7

The number of planets in Krypton's solar system.

ORBITING A RED SUN far from Earth, the doomed planet of Krypton was the birthplace of Superman and Supergirl. They were both sent to Earth to escape the planet's destruction. On Earth, Kryptonians have awesome powers, including super-strength and heightened senses.

INFO BLAST

CRIPPLING KRYPTONITE

Krypton was destroyed when its radioactive core caused it to explode. This created a material called Kryptonite, which is poisonous to Kryptonians. Superman's enemies soon discovered Kryptonite's effects, and stockpiled it to use against him.

POWERS
KRYPTONIANS

Powered by our yellow sun, Kryptonians have incredible powers while they are on Earth. Their super-strength lets them lift heavy objects with ease. They can also shoot heat from their eyes with their heat vision, leap long distances, and fly.

WHETHER THEY ARE faster than a speeding bullet or able to leap over tall buildings with a single bound, the Super Heroes have a diverse range of superpowers. Check out the incredible abilities of Earth's greatest heroes!

WOW!

Because Plastic Man's brain is not made of organic material, he is immune to telepathy. Not even Martian Manhunter can read his mind.

POWERS / SUPER HEROES

	SUPER-STRENGTH	SUPER-SPEED	FLIGHT	INVULNERABILITY	X-RAY VISION	FREEZE BREATH	HEAT VISION	SHAPE SHIFTING	TELEPATHY	ANIMAL CONTROL	INVISIBILITY	MASTERY OF MAGNETISM	TIME TRAVEL	ENERGY BOLTS
AQUAMAN	●	●		●					●	●				
BEAST BOY								●						
COSMIC BOY			●									●		
CYBORG	●	●	●					●						
THE FLASH		●									●		●	
GREEN LANTERN		●	●	●										
HAWKMAN	●		●											
LIGHTNING LAD			●											●
MARTIAN MANHUNTER	●	●	●	●				●	●		●			
PLASTIC MAN	●			●				●						
SHAZAM	●	●	●											
STARFIRE			●											●
SUPERMAN	●	●	●	●	●	●	●							
WONDER WOMAN	●	●	●	●										●

UNIVERSE IN UNITS

500,000

tons—the weight of the key to Superman's Fortress of Solitude. His super-strength lets him lift it with ease!

WHAT'S IN A NAME?

Ever wondered what Shazam's name means? It spells out his spectacular abilities!

S = THE WISDOM OF **S**OLOMON
H = THE STRENGTH OF **H**ERCULES
A = THE STAMINA OF **A**TLAS
Z = THE POWER OF **Z**EUS
A = THE INVULNERABILITY OF **A**CHILLES
M = THE SPEED OF **M**ERCURY

Q&A

HOW MANY SUPERPOWERS DOES BATMAN HAVE?

Absolutely none! Batman has trained his body and mind to be the best they can be, but he has no actual superpowers.

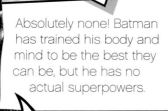

I DON'T NEED POWERS TO BE THE BEST. I'M BATMAN!

TOP 3
WEAKNESSES

KRYPTONITE
1 These radioactive rocks are all that's left of the planet Krypton. They strip Superman of his powers.

THE COLOR YELLOW
2 The Green Lantern's power ring gives him incredible powers, but it has no effect on anything yellow.

BATTERY POWER
3 If Cyborg doesn't remember to regularly charge himself, a low battery will wear him down!

SECRET

WHO IS THAT MASKED MAN? Heroes like Batman and Superman usually try to keep their real identities a closely guarded secret. It means that they can live a normal life away from the spotlight... if you can ever have a normal life as a Super Hero!

CLASSIC LOOK
A Super Hero's costume is key to hiding his or her true identity. Superman has had many costumes over the years. The first, in light-blue and red, made its debut in 2011.

THE NEW BLACK
Superman sported a moody look in 2013 in a rare black and chrome costume. The black suit helps him to absorb more sunlight for extra power.

BACK TO BLUE
Superman donned a dark blue suit and a new Utility Belt with gold pouches in 2016. He also gained a new hairstyle.

THE CHANGING STYLE OF **SUPERMAN**

Hinged doors allow for a swift costume change in the Batcave

INFO BLAST

BECOMING THE BAT
Billionaire Bruce Wayne has dedicated his life to fighting crime. After years of traveling the world to train his body and mind, Bruce returned to Gotham City and became Batman. When danger strikes, he heads down to the Batcave (from set 7783) to change into his Batsuit.

HEROES IN NUMBERS

1,075 bricks
Included in The Batcave: The Penguin and Mr. Freeze's Invasion (set 7783)

3 capes
Have been worn by Superman minifigures—two in red and one in black

1 movie
Features an exclusive Clark Kent minifigure—LEGO *Batman The Movie, DC Super Heroes Unite*

IDENTITIES

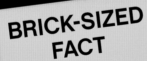

STAT SCAN

NAME:	Batman
REAL NAME:	Bruce Wayne
FRIENDS:	Robin, Superman
FOES:	Too many to mention
LIKES:	Working alone
DISLIKES:	Admitting he needs help

WHO HAS THE MOST NAMES...

SUPERMAN OR BATMAN?

SUPERMAN
- SUPERMAN
- CLARK KENT
- KAL-EL
- THE MAN OF STEEL
- THE LAST SON OF KRYPTON
- THE MAN OF TOMORROW

BATMAN
- BATMAN
- BRUCE WAYNE
- THE DARK KNIGHT DETECTIVE
- THE CAPED CRUSADER

SUPERMAN WINS ✓

CLARK KENT
Superman disguises himself as reporter Clark Kent by slipping on a pair of glasses. Only Lois Lane and Batman have worked out his secret... so far.

BARRY ALLEN
Few people know the true identity of the Fastest Man Alive. When he's not fighting crime as The Flash, Barry Allen works for the Central City police force.

DIANA PRINCE
Amazon princess Diana doesn't bother with the hassle of maintaining a secret identity. Everyone knows she's Wonder Woman!

GUESS WHO?

23

ALL IN THE FAMILY

SUPERMAN?

BEING A SUPER HERO is about more than just having powers. For many of the Justice League, a good upbringing instills a strong sense of what is right or wrong—and sometimes superpowered relatives can make all the difference in a fight!

WELL DONE, ROBIN

STEP ONE
Take DNA from Superman

STEP TWO
Take DNA from Lex Luthor

STEP THREE
Mix them together in a big cloning machine

STEP FOUR
Stand back and admire your handiwork. Superboy gets his powers from Superman and his arrogance from Lex!

INFO BLAST

ADOPTED FAMILY
An orphan himself, Batman takes in the young orphan Robin and trains him as his sidekick. Now, Robin looks up to Batman as a father figure—although the Boy Wonder sometimes thinks he knows best.

HEROES IN NUMBERS

45 minifigures
Share the same dark-brown hair piece as Jor-El, including Green Lantern

16 years old
Superboy was created to look like a 16-year-old version of Superman

1 set
Includes Superboy—he appears in an exclusive minifigure set for the retailer Target (set 5004076)

AWESOME!
The "S" on Superman and Supergirl's chests is the family crest of the El family. It means "hope" on Krypton.

INFO BLAST

LIKE FATHER, LIKE SON

Ever wondered why Superman is so brave? He gets it from his dad! When Jor-El realized that Krypton was going to explode, he sent his son to Earth in a rocket. He knew the Earth's sun would give Superman incredible powers!

KRYPTONIAN FAMILY TREE

KRYPTONIAN MOTHER	KRYPTONIAN FATHER	KRYPTONIAN UNCLE	KRYPTONIAN AUNT
Kara	Jor-El	Zor-El	Alura

SUPERMAN

COUSIN
Supergirl

CLONE
Superboy

STAT SCAN

NAME:	Supergirl
REAL NAME:	Kara Zor-El
FRIENDS:	Superman, Jimmy Olsen, Batgirl
FOES:	Brainiac
ABILITIES:	Flight, super-strength, super-speed, heat vision, X-ray vision
LIKES:	Exploring her powers
DISLIKES:	Being told what to do

SECRET ORIGIN

Kara was sent to Earth to look after her baby cousin. Unfortunately, her spaceship was knocked off course. By the time she finally arrived, her cousin had grown up to become Superman! Oops!

BRICK-SIZED FACT

Superman's family tree is so mysterious that three of the members are unknown to the LEGO DC Super Heroes universe.

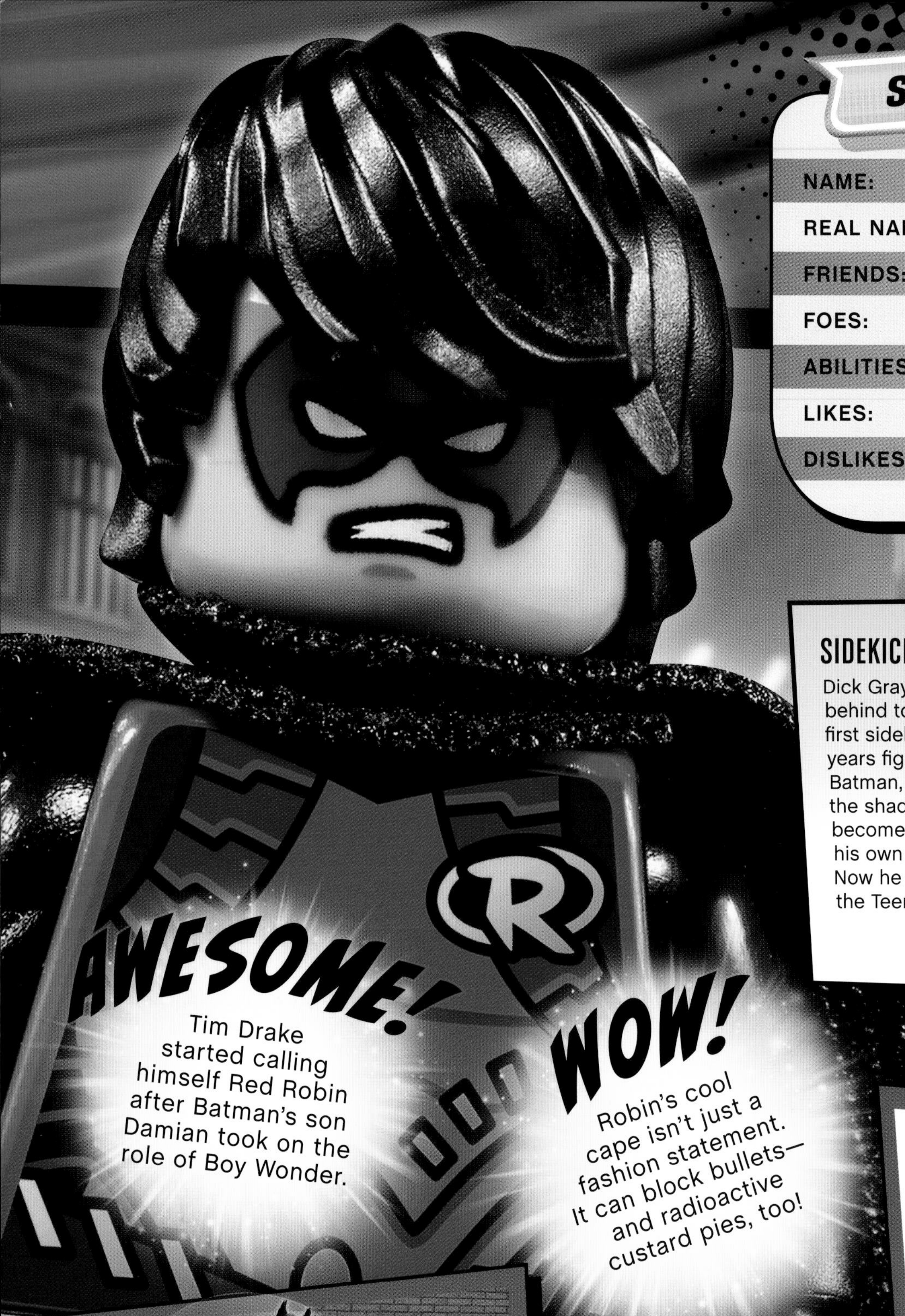

STAT SCAN

NAME:	Robin
REAL NAME:	Tim Drake
FRIENDS:	Batman, Alfred, Batgirl
FOES:	The Penguin, Bane, the Joker
ABILITIES:	Puzzle solving
LIKES:	Flying jets
DISLIKES:	Not being taken seriously

SIDEKICK NO MORE

Dick Grayson left the circus behind to become Batman's first sidekick. After a few years fighting alongside Batman, he stepped out of the shadow of the bat to become a Super Hero in his own right—Nightwing! Now he fights evil with the Teen Titans.

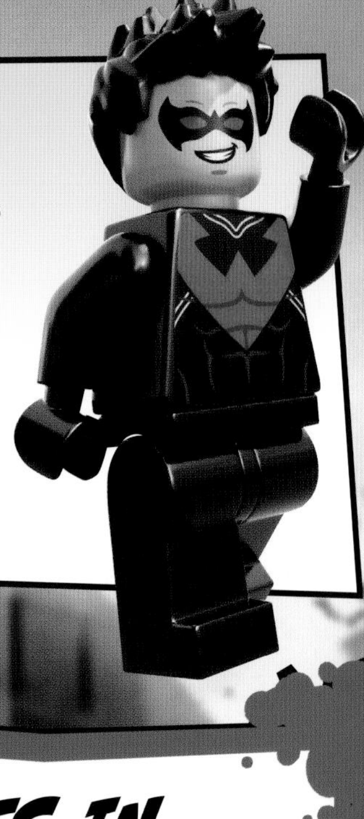

AWESOME!

Tim Drake started calling himself Red Robin after Batman's son Damian took on the role of Boy Wonder.

WOW!

Robin's cool cape isn't just a fashion statement. It can block bullets—and radioactive custard pies, too!

HEROES IN NUMBERS

5 LEGO vehicles
Have been piloted by Robin, including his scuba jet (from set 7885)

3 versions
Of Nightwing's minifigure have been made—two don a blue-and-black costume and one wears red and black

1 minifigure
Of Batgirl has been released so far

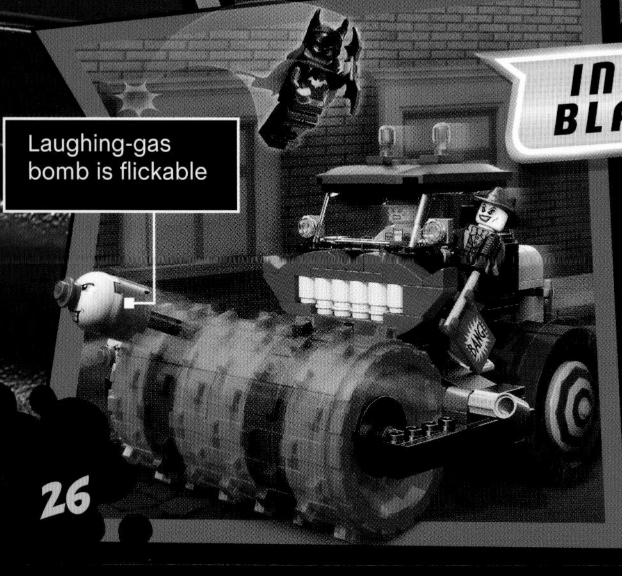

Laughing-gas bomb is flickable

INFO BLAST

GIRL WONDER

Batgirl is always ready to give the Dynamic Duo a hand. She doesn't hesitate to join them to stop the Joker in Batman: The Joker Steam Roller (set 76013). No one knows Batgirl is really Commissioner Gordon's daughter, Barbara!

HEROIC SIDEKICKS

BRICK-SIZED FACT

Damian Wayne made his first minifigure appearance as Robin in Batman: The Joker Steam Roller (set 76013).

SOMETIMES TWO SUPER HEROES are better than one. Even a loner like Batman needs a sidekick by his side—such as Robin, the Boy Wonder. Four young heroes have filled the role of Robin over the years, helping Batman on his missions and learning from his expertise.

DOs AND DON'Ts FOR...

ROBIN

DO...

- Always make Batman look good.
- Look before you leap into battle.
- Have a witty one-liner up your sleeve.

DON'T...

- Crash the Batmobile.
- Get captured over and over and over again.
- Ask "Why aren't you more like Superman?"
- Let on that you can work the Batcomputer better than Batman.

DICK GRAYSON
The first Robin was a circus performer who used his acrobatic skills to fight crime.

JASON TODD
Batman's second sidekick would go on to become the hot-headed anti-hero, Red Hood.

TIM DRAKE
Inquisitive Tim Drake worked out Batman's secret identity and volunteered for the job of Robin.

DAMIAN WAYNE
The latest Robin is Batman's son! He was trained by a league of ninjas from an early age.

MEET THE BOY WONDERS
Four different Robins have helped the Dark Knight.

FRIENDS AND ALLIES

IT'S EASY TO BE BRAVE when you have superpowers, but what about the "ordinary" people who risk life and limb to help their heroes? Let's celebrate the courageous chums of Earth's champions.

INFO BLAST

HARDY BY NAME...
U.S. Air Force Colonel Nathan Hardy led the defense against a Kryptonian invasion in Superman: Battle of Smallville (set 76003). Hardy didn't trust Superman at first, but he soon realized that Superman was fighting for truth and justice.

Rotating cannon with dual flick missiles

Commissioner Gordon has dedicated his life to putting super-villains behind bars. But Gotham is a dangerous place—poor Gordon has been kidnapped more times than any other police officer in the history of law enforcement!

Q&A
WHAT'S IT LIKE TO BE GOTHAM CITY'S TOP COP?

One mystery still eludes Gordon—who is the Caped Crusader? What would he think if he knew his friend Bruce Wayne is Batman, or that his own daughter is Batgirl?

STAT SCAN

NAME:	James Gordon
FRIENDS:	Bruce Wayne
FOES:	Every criminal in Gotham City
LIKES:	Law and order
DISLIKES:	Bad guys escaping justice

HEROES IN NUMBERS

517 bricks
Included in Heroes of Justice: Sky High Battle (set 76046), which Lois Lane appears in

12 minifigures
Have the same long red hair as Lois Lane's minifigure

2 versions
Of Lois Lane minifigures exist (so far!)

GUTSY LOIS
Lois didn't think twice when she sneaked onboard General Zod's ship to help her boyfriend in Superman: Black Zero Escape (set 76009). Little did she know she'd soon be trapped in an escape pod hurtling toward Earth!

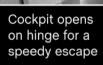

Cockpit opens on hinge for a speedy escape

TOP 5
FACTS ABOUT LOIS LANE

1 She is the *Daily Planet*'s number-one journalist. Brave Lois will stop at nothing to get a top story.

2 Lois was the reporter who first gave Superman his name.

3 Her dad is General Sam Lane, head of Area 52. This top-secret army base is used to store dangerous alien tech.

4 There's one secret Lois will never reveal—that Superman is really her boyfriend, Clark Kent!

5 A freak accident once gave Lois all Clark's powers. She soon took to the skies as Superwoman!

BRICK-SIZED FACT
Colonel Hardy, Commissioner Gordon, and the two Lois Lane minifigures are all exclusive to just one set each.

STAT SCAN

NAME:	Lois Lane
FRIENDS:	Clark Kent, Jimmy Olsen
FOES:	Lex Luthor
LIKES:	Getting exclusives
DISLIKES:	Losing a scoop

JUSTICE LEAGUE

WHEN ONE HERO isn't enough, Earth's champions join forces to form the Justice League. As the planet's last line of defense, the League have fought the universe's worst villains, stopped alien invasions, and inspired generations of Super Hero fans!

AWESOME!

Cyborg's password for the Justice League computer is "BatFan1"!

THE WATCHTOWER

The Justice League look out for danger on Earth by observing satellite feeds in their space headquarters. This high-tech space station also includes a prison and space to store hazardous material, such as Kryptonite.

UNIVERSE IN UNITS

5

The number of LEGO sets to feature Justice League team-ups so far.

BATTY BAT-MITE

Batman wasn't happy about joining the Justice League at first. He felt he worked better alone (don't tell Robin!). That was until Bat-Mite arrived on the scene. When this strange interdimensional creature kidnapped the League, Batman realized he had no option but to join their ranks.

BRICK-SIZED FACT

Bat-Mite appears in the television special LEGO DC Comics: Batman Be-Leagured.

JUSTICE LEAGUE

RULEBOOK

✓ Secret identities are not to be mentioned while in costume.

✓ Always wear your seatbelt in the Javelin.

✓ Never keep spare Kryptonite in your back pocket. In fact, don't keep it in your front pocket either!

"DON'T RAISE YOUR HAND AT ALL UNTIL YOU'VE FIRST EXTENDED IT."

STRANGE

Superman didn't use his X-ray vision to see through Batman's mask. Instead, he noticed that Alfred had stitched Bruce Wayne's name into the back of Batman's pants!

SELF-MADE SUPER HEROES

WHO NEEDS SUPERPOWERS? Not Green Arrow or Batman! Aided by their family fortunes, they have taught themselves incredible skills in order to become lean, mean, fighting machines. Now, they rub shoulders with the most powerful heroes on the planet.

INFO BLAST

HEROES IN NUMBERS

4,000 calories
Are consumed by Batman every day to survive his grueling crime-fighting career

127 martial arts
Have been mastered by the Dark Knight

1 minifigure
Wields the LEGO bow and arrow in green—Green Arrow, of course!

BRICK-SIZED FACT
Before he appeared in Darkseid Invasion (set 76028), Green Arrow was only available as an exclusive minifigure at a 2013 Comic-Con.

ALL OF A QUIVER
Green Arrow doesn't have any superpowers. Instead, he has trained his body to become the ultimate weapon, mastering countless martial arts and, of course, archery skills.

THE SMART KNIGHT
When it comes to fighting crime, Batman's brain is just as important as his biceps. The Caped Crusader always needs to think one step ahead of Gotham's villains in order to outwit them. He's trained himself to excel in everything from coding to chemistry.

DETECTING   MARTIAL ARTS   SCIENCE   ACROBATICS   MARKSMANSHIP   ESCAPING TRACKS   SMILING

BATMAN'S SKILLS

STAT SCAN

NAME:	Green Arrow
REAL NAME:	Oliver Queen
FRIENDS:	His sidekick, Arsenal
FOES:	Deathstroke
LIKES:	Hitting the target
DISLIKES:	Running out of arrows

UNIVERSE IN UNITS

29

The number of arrows Green Arrow can shoot every minute.

WOW!

Green Arrow began his training when he was shipwrecked on a remote island. He needed to be in peak condition to survive the harsh environment.

Q&A

WHO HAS THE MOST CASH TO SPEND ON FIGHTING CRIME?

1 Oliver Queen, a.k.a. Green Arrow, is head of Queen Industries and helped fund the founding of the Justice League. He's worth a staggering seven billion dollars!

2 Bruce Wayne, as head of Wayne Enterprises, is worth 80 billion dollars! Well, somebody has to pay for all those Batmobiles, Batplanes, and Batboats.

33

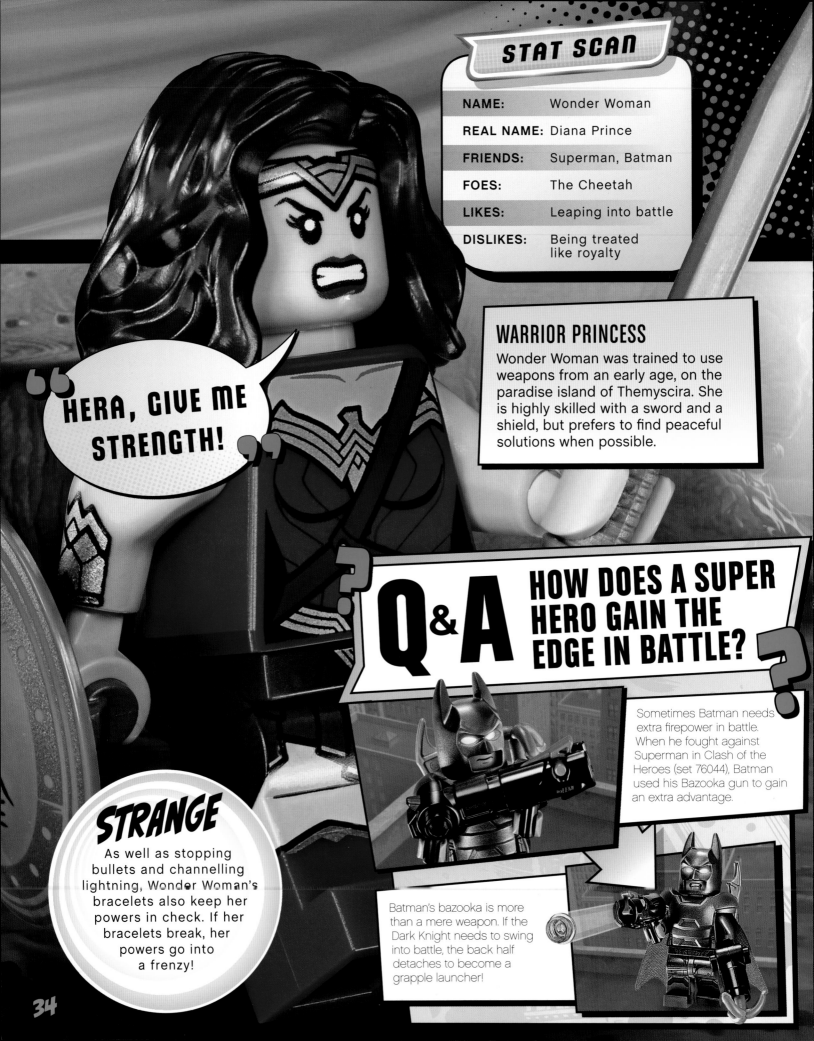

NAME:	Wonder Woman
REAL NAME:	Diana Prince
FRIENDS:	Superman, Batman
FOES:	The Cheetah
LIKES:	Leaping into battle
DISLIKES:	Being treated like royalty

"HERA, GIVE ME STRENGTH!"

WARRIOR PRINCESS

Wonder Woman was trained to use weapons from an early age, on the paradise island of Themyscira. She is highly skilled with a sword and a shield, but prefers to find peaceful solutions when possible.

STRANGE

As well as stopping bullets and channelling lightning, Wonder Woman's bracelets also keep her powers in check. If her bracelets break, her powers go into a frenzy!

Q&A HOW DOES A SUPER HERO GAIN THE EDGE IN BATTLE?

Sometimes Batman needs extra firepower in battle. When he fought against Superman in Clash of the Heroes (set 76044), Batman used his Bazooka gun to gain an extra advantage.

Batman's bazooka is more than a mere weapon. If the Dark Knight needs to swing into battle, the back half detaches to become a grapple launcher!

WONDERFUL WEAPONS

BRICK-SIZED FACT

Batman's Batarang has appeared in more than 30 sets—usually in black, but occasionally in silver.

ALTHOUGH SUPER HEROES prefer to rely on their superpowers or martial arts skills, sometimes they need a little extra help from their weapons. The heroes train for years to master their weapon of choice, from razor-sharp swords to spinning Batarangs!

INFO BLAST

KATANA'S SWORD

Japanese warrior Tatsu Yamashiro, a.k.a. Katana, is a skilled swordswoman, second only to Wonder Woman. Trained by a samurai, Katana wields a magical sword called the Soultaker. She's even been known to chop carrots with it.

TOP 6 WEAPONS

1 BATARANG

Batman uses his personalized bat-shaped boomerangs to knock out villains from long distances.

2 LASSO OF TRUTH

Wonder Woman's magical glowing lasso forces anyone who gets caught in it to tell the truth!

3 BOW AND ARROWS

Green Arrow and Arsenal always carry a supply of arrows. The talented archers never miss a target.

4 BLASTER

Cyborg carries his blaster gun with him at all times. It fires deadly lasers with pinpoint precision.

5 THANAGARIAN MACE

Hawkman's whirling weapon is made from a dense alien metal called Nth metal.

6 QUARTERSTAFF

Robin uses his trusty staff as part of his fighting style. It helps him block attacks from his enemies.

UNIVERSE IN UNITS

30

The number of LEGO sets to feature the sword Katana's minifigure holds.

SIMPLE DESIGN
When he started out, Batman's belt was relatively simple, designed mainly to hold up Batman's pants.

STORAGE SPACE
Over time, the Dark Knight added pockets and pouches to his belt so he could carry all his cool gadgets.

HIGH-TECH
Modern Utility Belts include new high-tech features, such as remote controls for the Batmobile.

ROBIN'S BELT
Batman isn't the only hero to have a Utility Belt. Robin has one built directly into his body armor.

PROGRESSION OF THE UTILITY BELT

TOP 5
THINGS TO KEEP IN YOUR UTILITY BELT

1 SHARK REPELLENT SPRAY
You never know when you might be attacked by a great white. Barracuda, whale, and manta ray repellents are also available.

2 SMOKE CAPSULES
These handy smoke capsules are perfect if you need to hide—no villain will be able to spot you in a thick smoke cloud.

3 NET
What do you do if The Flash is being menaced by vicious villains? You trap the unsuspecting crooks in your handy net, that's what!

4 DETECTIVE KIT
As the World's Greatest Detective, you need to carry detective equipment at all times. Don't leave your Batcave without a microscope and fingerprint kit.

5 BAT BEACON
This is ideal if you need to confuse a criminal. Hit the Bat Beacon and an ultrasonic homing signal will attract swarms of bats to send them into a flap.

UNIVERSE IN UNITS 170
Cyborg's IQ. He's a genius even without his built-in computer!

INFO BLAST

NO MORE LIES
The Batcave (from set 76052) contains all kinds of gadgets, including Batman's lie detector machine. It can easily tell if a foul feline felon is telling a fib—and that's the truth!

GEAR AND GADGETS

FIGHTING CRIME ISN'T JUST about using amazing powers or incredible weapons. Justice League members have gathered a large collection of gizmos and gadgets—from Batman's Utility Belt to Cyborg's entire body!

STRANGE

Cyborg's head can come off and fly around on a neck rocket. Weird!

BRICK-SIZED FACT

Cyborg's special head mold was created just for him. It fits over his very smiley minifigure head.

POWERS

CYBORG

Cyborg, whose real name is Victor Stone, is a walking gadget! He has built-in blasters, rocket boosters, a computer, and remote danger sensors. Let's hope that Victor remembers to recharge himself—a flat battery drains him of his powers!

Body armor strong enough to withstand energy attacks

Infrared and thermal sensor

Legs contain jump jets to leap great heights

STAT SCAN

NAME:	Cyborg
REAL NAME:	Victor Stone
FRIENDS:	Superman, Supergirl
FOES:	Darkseid, Brainiac
LIKES:	His hero, Batman
DISLIKES:	Getting a flat battery

COSTUMES AND ARMOR

When the going gets tough, the tough pull on armor. From granting special powers to protecting a hero in conflict, a high-tech suit is more than just a fashion statement!

SCARAB POWER

Blue Beetle's armor is created by a magical scarab connected to Jaime's spine! His armor comes with jet packs and energy cannons, and can also translate any language in the universe!

BRICK-SIZED FACT

Blue Beetle's transparent blue wings and Hawkman's golden wings were both specially created for their minifigures.

STAT SCAN

NAME:	Blue Beetle
REAL NAME:	Jaime Reyes
FRIENDS:	The Teen Titans
FOES:	Killer Moth
LIKES:	Working in a team
DISLIKES:	Being treated like a kid

INFO BLAST

Net shooter and two stud shooters for extra firepower

BAT-MECH

Batman was forced to use this giant robot armor to take down Superman after the Man of Steel was brainwashed by Brainiac in Gorilla Grodd Goes Bananas (set 76026). He shone highly concentrated sunlight from the armor's glowing Bat-Signal to restore Superman's senses!

STRANGE

Just in case Bruce Wayne is ever transported back in time, the Batmobile comes stocked with caveman costumes and even a pirate outfit!

THE CHANGING STYLE OF...

ORIGINAL HERO
Wonder Woman's 2012 debut costume is based on the stars and stripes of the US flag. Her hair and tiara are one piece.

SILVER REBOOT
Diana's minifigure donned a new costume in 2015 after her outfit was ruined by the Trickster's stink bomb! She swapped her gold tiara for silver.

AMAZONIAN WARRIOR
In 2016, Wonder Woman sported Amazonian armor, complete with a strap for her shield and sword, and awesome bulletproof bracelets.

EXCLUSIVE MINIFIGURE
Wonder Woman said good-bye to her old look for the minifigure that comes with this book. Her new costume has long sleeves and pants.

UNIVERSE IN UNITS

21

The number of sets that contain the Bat-Mech's wings.

STAT SCAN

NAME:	Hawkman
REAL NAME:	Katar Hol
FRIENDS:	Hawkgirl
FOES:	Doctor Hastor
LIKES:	Flying off the handle
DISLIKES:	Keeping his temper in check

AWESOME!
Hawkman's gravity-defying battle suit is made of Nth metal. It's this lighter-than-air alloy that allows him to fly like a bird!

39

ACCIDENTALLY AWESOME

Not all Super Heroes are born with unbelievable powers. Some get their incredible abilities by accident. Luckily, The Flash, Beast Boy, and Plastic Man all chose to use their newfound gifts for good rather than bad!

WOW!
Beast Boy doesn't just become modern-day creatures. He can change into giant dinosaurs too!

POWERS

BEAST BOY

ANIMAL MAGIC

When Garfield Logan contracted a rare tropical disease as a child, his parents gave him a miracle cure. This magical medicine had an unexpected side effect. Now, Garfield can transform into any animal he has ever seen!

BRICK-SIZED FACT

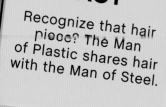

Recognize that hair piece? The Man of Plastic shares hair with the Man of Steel.

INFO BLAST

PLASTIC FANTASTIC

During a life-changing crime gone wrong, thief Patrick "Eel" O'Brian was doused in a concoction of weird and wonderful chemicals. Discovering he could stretch his body into any shape possible, Eel turned over a new leaf and became Plastic Man.

STAT SCAN

NAME:	Beast Boy
REAL NAME:	Garfield Logan
FRIENDS:	Robin, Starfire
FOES:	Deathstroke
LIKES:	Animals of all shapes and sizes
DISLIKES:	Being made a monkey

STAT SCAN

NAME:	The Flash
REAL NAME:	Barry Allen
FRIENDS:	Superman, Wonder Woman
FOES:	Captain Cold, General Grodd, Captain Boomerang
LIKES:	Playing tag
DISLIKES:	Stop signs

STRANGE

Thanks to his Speed Force, The Flash can vibrate his body so fast that he can run straight through LEGO bricks!

INFO BLAST

QUICK AS A FLASH

Barry Allen wasn't that fast until he was struck by lightning. Now powered by a mysterious energy known as the Speed Force, The Flash can move faster than any living being. He is so quick he can even race across oceans!

UNIVERSE IN UNITS

23,759,449,000,000,000,000,000,000,000,000,000,000,000,000,000

times the speed of light—the fastest The Flash has ever run!

NAME:	Green Lantern
REAL NAME:	Hal Jordan
FRIENDS:	Superman, Wonder Woman
FOES:	Sinestro
LIKES:	Flying
DISLIKES:	Showing fear

" IN BRIGHTEST DAY,
IN BLACKEST NIGHT,
NO EVIL SHALL
ESCAPE MY SIGHT.
LET THOSE WHO WORSHIP
EVIL'S MIGHT,
BEWARE MY POWER—
GREEN LANTERN'S LIGHT! "

GREEN LANTERN CORPS OATH

INFO BLAST

CUNNING CONSTRUCTS

Green Lantern has a special power ring, which allows him to create bright-green "constructs" of anything he can imagine. These can be as simple as a giant boxing glove or as complex as a spaceship, like the one he created in Green Lantern vs. Sinestro (set 76025).

AWESOME!

Hal isn't the only Green Lantern. Thousands of planets have their own emerald guardians, each with a power ring.

Spring-loaded missiles are fired by twisting the rear exhaust port

42

SPACE HEROES

Danger lurks everywhere, even in the deepest reaches of space. Fortunately, these awesome alien heroes and cosmic-powered champions are always ready to protect the universe!

ALIEN ALLIES

MARTIAN MANHUNTER
A native of Mars, Martian Manhunter can disguise himself as any hero. He can also control minds!

STARFIRE
A princess from the planet Tamaran, Starfire can fire starbolt energy from her hands.

SUPERMAN
People often forget that the Man of Steel is a strange visitor from another planet himself!

SPACE BATMAN
The Dark Knight can survive in space—thanks to his armor, rocket pack, mechanical bat wings, and breathing apparatus. He wears this to battle Sinestro in Green Lantern vs. Sinestro (set 76025).

BRICK-SIZED FACT
The Space Batman minifigure comes with two head pieces (one with a mask and one with two facial expressions) and two sets of wings (folded in and folded out).

UNIVERSE IN UNITS
7,200+
The number of Green Lanterns operating across the universe.

THINGS ARE GETTING A LITTLE FISHY AROUND HERE!

STAT SCAN

NAME:	Aquaman
REAL NAME:	Arthur Curry
FRIENDS:	Superman, Batman, lots of fish
FOES:	Black Manta
LIKES:	Swimming
DISLIKES:	Water pollution

INFO BLAST

LORD OF THE SEA

As King of Atlantis, Aquaman is the protector of Earth's oceans. The half-human, half-Atlantean hero is able to communicate telepathically with any sea creature. He is also a proud member of the Justice League.

SCUBA BATMAN

Batman loses his cape to take a swim in full scuba gear. He swaps Batarangs for a harpoon to fight the Penguin in Batman: The Penguin Face Off (set 76010).

UNDERWATER ROBIN

In a scuba suit and mask, the Boy Wonder takes a plunge with Aquaman to battle Black Manta in Black Manta Deep Sea Strike (set 76027).

THE DEEP-SEA DUO

MAKE A SPLASH

Underwater Super Hero Aquaman protects the planet's oceans from harm. Many dangers lurk in the ocean's depths, but Aquaman can always count on Earth's heroes to dive into the deep when he needs their help in battle.

BRICK-SIZED FACT

The trident that Aquaman holds is found in 22 LEGO sets, across eight different themes.

UNIVERSE IN UNITS

145,000+

The number of years ago that the city of Atlantis was founded.

TOP 4
WATERPROOF WONDERS

1 BATBOAT
Batman and Robin's catamaran (from set 76034) splits into two separate hovercrafts and comes with a radar tower to track down enemy vessels.

2 BAT SUB
Slicing easily through the water, the deep-sea Bat sub (from set 76027) has a detachable micro-sub, which is ideal for diving into narrow sea caves.

3 SCUBA SPEEDER
Batman's scuba vehicle (from set 76010) is small enough to avoid being detected by the Penguin's radar scope. Its twin torpedoes also pack a powerful punch.

4 SCUBA JET
Robin's speedy Scuba Jet (from set 7885) is ideal for pursuing crooks making an underwater getaway. Robin thinks its bright colors are seriously stylish, too.

SECRET HIDEAWAYS

Where do Super Heroes go when they need time alone? Their top secret hideaway, of course. There are lots of different Super Hero hideaways, but the most famous is the Batcave, Batman's underground control center. It's full of cutting-edge, crime-fighting technology—and lots of bats.

HEROES IN NUMBERS

2,526 bricks

Included in the Batman Classic TV Series—Batcave (set 76052)

1007 Mountain Drive

The address of Wayne Manor

4 sets

Feature the Batcave (so far!)

The Batcopter can land on the helipad

SUBTERRANEAN BASE

The Batcave (set 76052) houses everything that the Dark Knight needs to combat crime. There's an atomic-powered laboratory, plus space for a whole fleet of vehicles, including the Batcycle, Batcopter, and the Batmobile!

Batman's lie detector machine helps him interrogate crooks

Q&A

HOW DO YOU ENTER THE BATCAVE?

A secret panel will open, revealing the Batpoles. Grab on to the handles and don't look down!

After receiving a call to action from Commissioner Gordon, tilt the bust of Shakespeare on Bruce's desk and press the red button.

Slide down the poles, changing into your Super Hero costume on the way. The poles are fitted with rocket elevators to take you back up to the Manor.

INFO BLAST

FORTRESS OF SOLITUDE

Set in a remote location, Superman's Fortress of Solitude provides him with a secure base to plan his missions. The secret location and high security means Superman can come here to think without fear of being interrupted.

STAT SCAN

NAME:	Alfred Pennyworth
FRIENDS:	Bruce Wayne, Dick Grayson
FOES:	Dust
LIKES:	Looking after Master Bruce
DISLIKES:	Things being out of place

LOYAL SERVANT

Batman's loyal butler, Alfred, not only cooks all of Batman's meals, he also keeps the Batcave spick and span. He even repairs the Batmobile when it gets damaged.

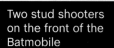

Two stud shooters on the front of the Batmobile

DEFENDING THE SKIES

WHILE SUPERMAN NEEDS no help to head up, up, and away, other heroes rely on astonishing aircraft to take to the skies. From Wonder Woman's Invisible Jet to Batman's armored Batwing, the sky's the limit with these incredible planes.

Spring-loaded missile

Q&A HOW DO YOU SURPRISE A VILLAIN?

Approach in the Invisible Jet. Try not to make a sound—the jet itself is invisible, but it doesn't make its pilot invisible too.

Set your sights on the bad guys and swoop down from the sky! If you're lucky, they won't see you coming!

TOP 3
ACE AIRCRAFT

THE JAVELIN
1 The Justice League's sleek starship, the Javelin (from set 76028), can plunge beneath the waves, or soar into space.

THE BATWING
2 Batman's speedy Batwing (from set 76013) has moveable wings that can snap together to grab escaping villains!

CONSTRUCT SPACESHIP
3 Green Lantern created this spaceship (from set 76025) so he could fly to planet Korugar and take back his stolen lantern from Sinestro.

WHO'S IN THE DRIVER'S SEAT?
The Javelin was designed by Batman. It features a hidden hatch beneath the cockpit, which is ideal for launching attacks from above. Batman usually flies the Javelin himself as he believes he's the best pilot. Hal Jordan doesn't agree—he was an Air Force pilot before he became Green Lantern!

STRANGE

The Invisible Jet is actually an intelligent alien crystal that can become any type of vehicle!

AWESOME!

Wonder Woman can summon her Invisible Jet using her tiara's telepathic powers!

Transparent wing pieces were created especially for the Invisible Jet

SPEED · STEALTH · STYLE

VEHICLE VITALS

INFO BLAST

WINGED WARRIOR

Nightwing got his love of cool vehicles from Bruce Wayne. When Man-Bat was threatening Gotham City in Batman: Man-Bat Attack (set 76011), Nightwing used this glider to defeat him.

BRICK-SIZED FACT

If Nightwing ever flies into trouble, his glider (set 76011) has grapples that attach to the Batcopter so he can be towed to safety.

HEROES IN NUMBERS

34 clear bricks

Make up the Invisible Jet in Gorilla Grodd Goes Bananas (set 76026)

8 seats

For Justice League minifigures are included in the Javelin from Darkseid Invasion (set 76026)

4 flick missiles

Feature on the Batwing in Batman: The Joker Steam Roller (set 76013)

NEED FOR SPEED

NOT EVERYONE can race into action like The Flash. Batman and Robin have the coolest collection of cars and cycles, from the heavily armored Tumbler to the sleekest speeder of them all, the Batmobile.

STRANGE

Although these days he prefers black, Batman's very first Batmobile was bright red!

Windshield lifts up to allow Batman into the cockpit

BATMAN'S MOTORS

THE BATMOBILE

Batman's main set of wheels is the speedy Batmobile (from set 76045), complete with hidden weapons and a mobile crime lab.

THE BAT-TANK

Batman burst through the gates of Bane's heavily fortified hideout using this tank (from set 7787), with flick-fire missiles.

THE DRAGSTER

The Caped Crusader revealed his dart-like dragster (from set 7779) to chase down Catwoman on her CatCycle.

THE TUMBLER

The Tumbler (set 76023) was originally designed by Wayne Enterprises for the military. Its armor is strong enough to break through walls.

Twin stud shooters mounted on the front of the Batmobile

UNIVERSE IN UNITS

330

The Batmobile's top speed in miles per hour (530 in kilometers per hour).

HEROES IN NUMBERS

500,000
The number of LEGO bricks needed to build a full-sized Batmobile

1,045 bricks
Make up The Batmobile: Ultimate Collectors' Edition (set 7784), the largest LEGO Batmobile of them all

14 sets
Feature the Batmobile (so far!)

3 seconds
The time the Batmobile takes to accelerate from 0-60 mph (100 km/h)

TOP 3 BRILLIANT BIKES

1 BATCYCLE
The Batcycle (from set 76053) has built-in laser cannons and monster tires to zoom through even the narrowest gaps.

2 NIGHTWING'S BIKE
Dick Grayson's rocket-powered motorcycle (from set 7785) has space to store his two fighting sticks.

3 RED HOOD'S BIKE
Former Robin, Jason Todd, shows his loyalty to the Dark Knight by including the Bat Signal on his sleek two-wheeler (from set 76055).

STEALTH STYLE SPEED

VEHICLE VITALS

RIGHT PLACE, WRONG TIME

IT ISN'T EASY LIVING IN METROPOLIS or Gotham City. Some days, you can't step out of your door without a super-villain striking. Meet the ordinary people who get caught up in extraordinary events and ask yourself, what would you do if you were caught by a giant gorilla?

BRICK-SIZED FACT

No wonder the security guard minifigure is so brave—he shares his head piece with Bruce Wayne!

WHAT A SLIP-UP!

This poor truck driver was just trying to do his job, delivering fruit to the good people of Gotham, when Gorilla Grodd decided to steal his entire stock in Gorilla Grodd Goes Bananas (set 76026)!

Q&A

HOW DO I KEEP CALM IN A SUPER-VILLAIN CRISIS?

Take a leaf out of the book of Gotham City's number-one security guard. When Two-Face stole the bank vault, this brave bystander kept his head when all around were fleeing in terror. He raised the alarm, calling Batman personally.

Most people would have turned and run when the Batmobile arrived. Not this guy. He produced a spare pair of handcuffs, just in case the Caped Crusader needed help restraining Two-Face's goons.

Because of his bravery, he was offered the important job of guarding the prisoners at Arkham Asylum. He's perfect for the job—he stays calm even when the crooks try to escape!

AAAAAAARCH!

STAT SCAN

NAME:	Vic Timm
FRIENDS:	Anyone who saves him
FOES:	Telepathic gorillas and scary scarecrows
ABILITIES:	Driving trucks and farm equipment, running
LIKES:	Reliable vehicles
DISLIKES:	Super-villains

INFO BLAST

UNIVERSE IN UNITS

1

The number of LEGO sets the Gorilla Grodd figure appears in.

FEAR ON THE FARM

Things went from bad to worse for the banana truck driver. After his run-in with Grodd, he quit his job, moved away, and became a farmer in Smallville. He enjoyed his new life—until the Scarecrow put him in a tank of fear gas in Batman: Scarecrow Harvest of Fear (set 76054)!

DOS AND DON'Ts FOR...

BEING RESCUED

DO...

- Read *How To Be Rescued From Super-Villains and/or Aliens* by Lois Lane. It's a great read.
- Say "thank you." Good manners cost nothing!
- Sell your story to the *Daily Planet* as soon as possible afterward.

DON'T...

- Try to tell the Super Hero how to save you. They hate that (especially Batman).
- Forget to take a selfie with the Super Hero. Why not get one with the super-villain, too? This is your moment in the spotlight!
- Attempt to steal a Batarang or Lasso of Truth as a memento.

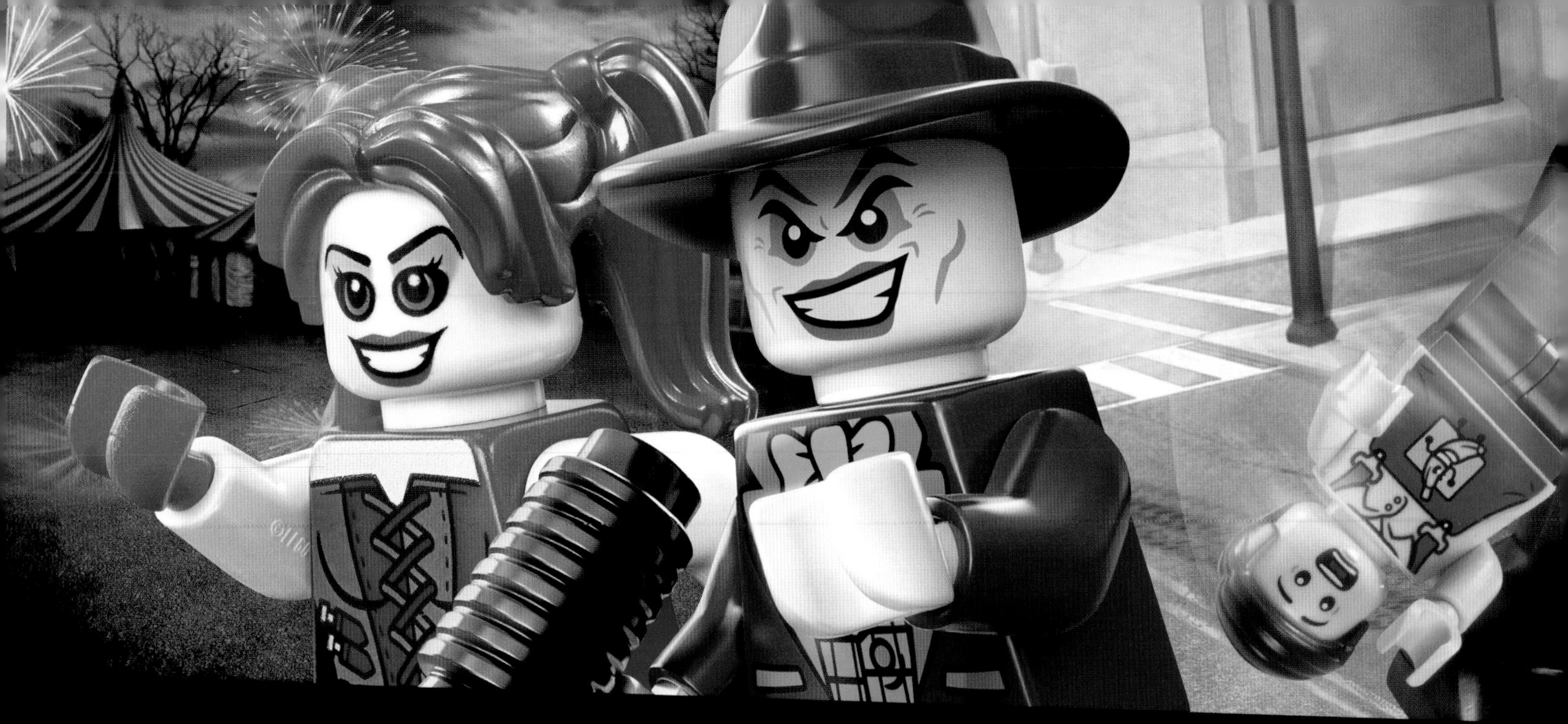

SUPER-

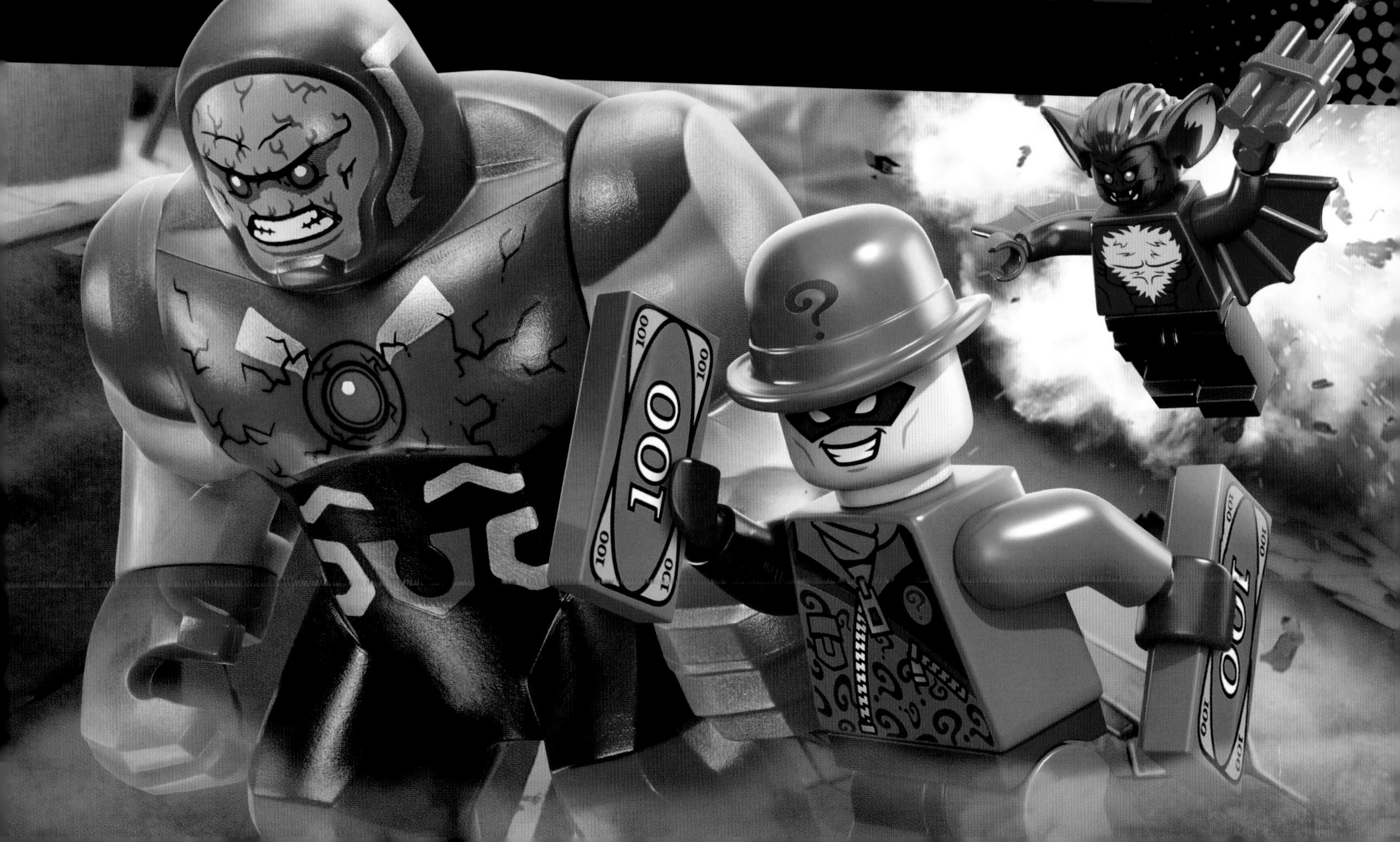
100

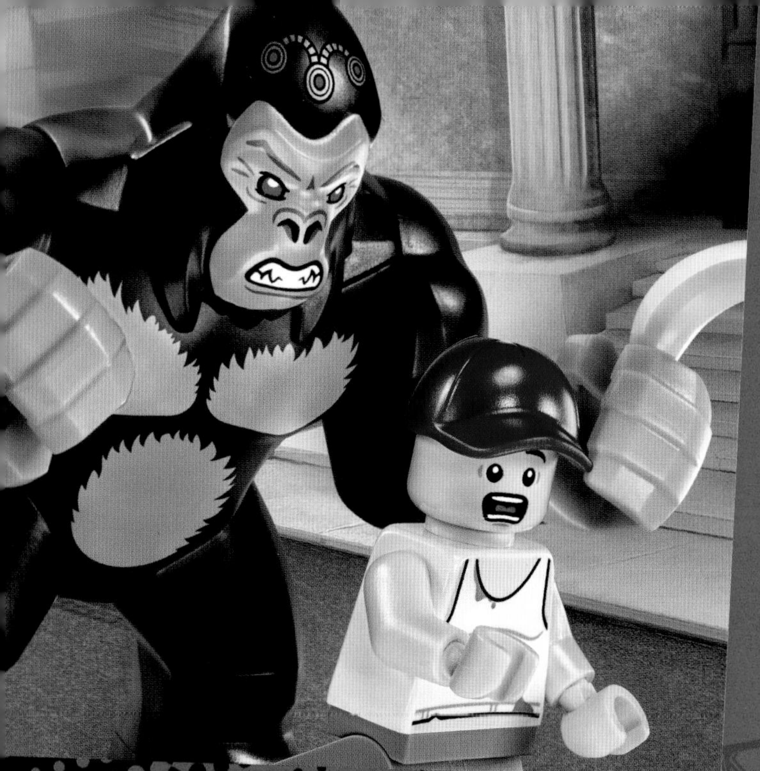

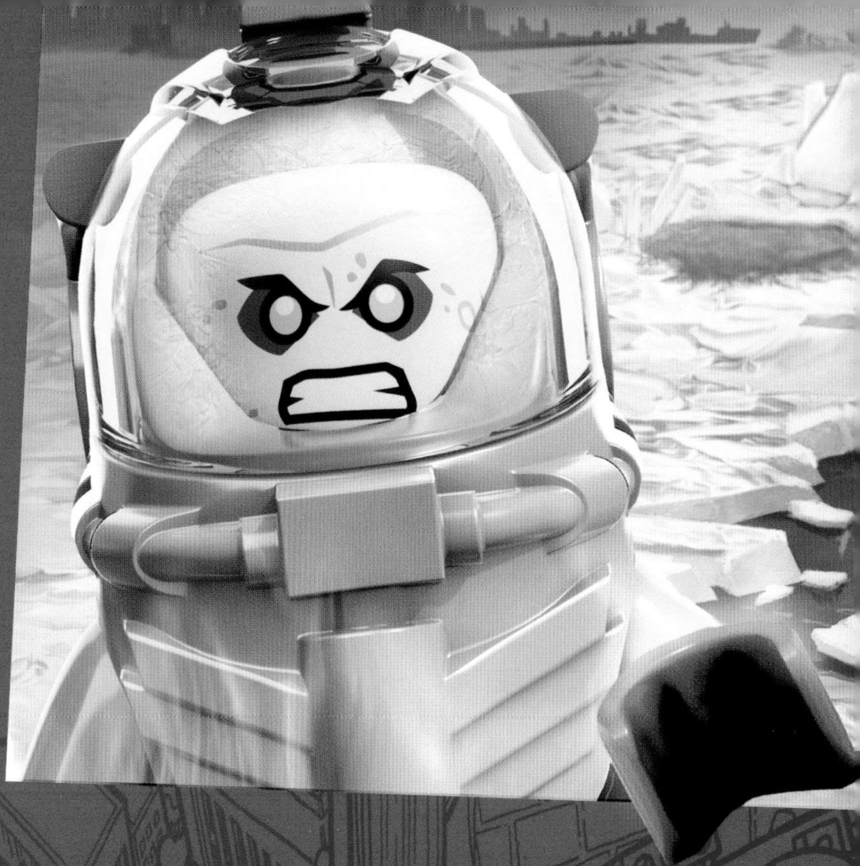

VILLAINS

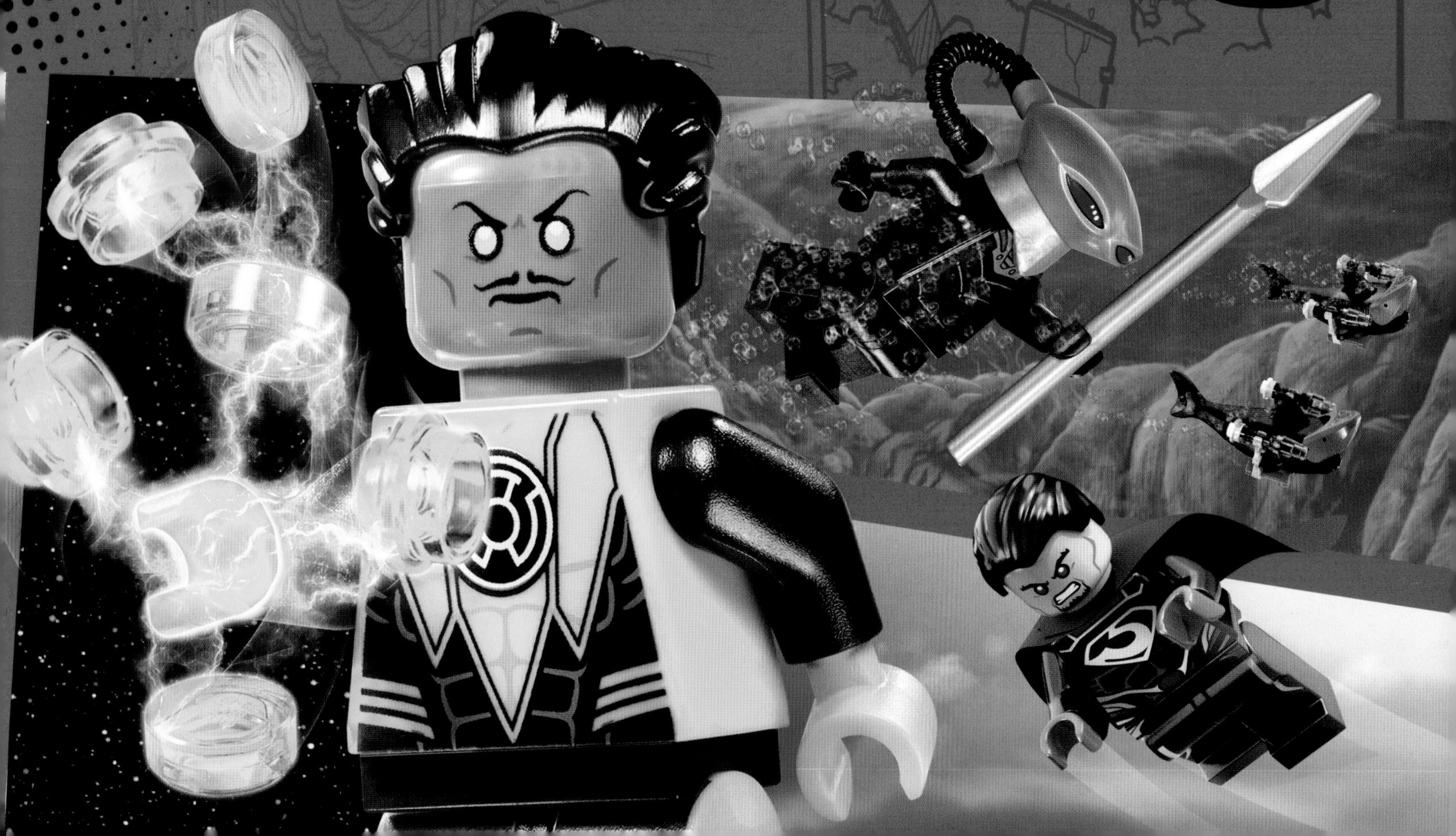

MEET THE VILLAINS

Boo! Hiss! Meet the wicked wrongdoers everyone loves to hate. These vile villains are evil to their core. Nothing in the world can stop their plans for universal domination... well, except for Superman and the Justice League, of course. Phew!

CATWOMAN
Gotham City's most infamous cat burglar can't resist stealing precious jewels.

MR. FREEZE
This subzero scoundrel performs crimes to fund his chilling experiments.

BIZARRO
Superman's befuddled clone often fights on the side of villainy—but he's not all bad.

POISON IVY
A vine-covered villainess, Poison Ivy will stop at nothing to protect the environment.

CAPTAIN BOOMERANG
This Australian thief keeps coming back again and again and again.

THE PENGUIN
This waddling crime lord rules the Gotham City underworld.

DEADSHOT
The straightest shooter around, Deadshot never misses his target.

GORILLA GRODD
Fruit sellers beware! This hairy hoodlum goes ape for bananas.

KILLER MOTH
Available for hire to any Gotham City villain, Killer Moth is an expert in martial arts.

LEX LUTHOR
A billionaire criminal genius, Lex poses as a pillar of the community—he even ran for president.

THE JOKER
Also known as the Clown Prince of Crime, the Joker is Batman's bonkers archenemy.

KILLER CROC
Half-human, half-crocodile, Killer Croc is a reptilian rascal from the New York sewers.

MAN-BAT
This villainous beast is the scourge of the night sky.

TWO-FACE
Once an upstanding attorney, Two-Face is now a Gotham gangster obsessed with chance.

DARKSEID
Not content with ruling planet Apokolips, this alien overlord now wants Earth.

DEATHSTROKE
A master mercenary, Deathstroke is eager to prove crime *does* pay.

THE RIDDLER
Which villain can't help but leave clues to his crimes? Why, the Riddler, of course.

SINESTRO
A Green Lantern turned bad, Sinestro now seeks to plunge the galaxy into the darkest night.

TRICKSTER
This crafty conman uses his talent for trickery and deception in his crimes.

BANE
Kept bulked-up by his secret stash of venom, Bane is a muscled mischief-maker.

CAPTAIN COLD
The world's coldest criminal, Captain Cold is also The Flash's biggest foe.

GENERAL ZOD
A crazed Kryptonian criminal, Zod won't rest until everyone kneels before him.

THE SCARECROW
Turning people's lives into nightmares with his fear gas, the Scarecrow is one frightening fiend.

HARLEY QUINN
This doctor turned villainous jester is a mischievous menace.

BRAINIAC
This hyper-intelligent living computer has a passion for collecting planets.

BLACK MANTA
Lurking under the sea, Black Manta is Aquaman's archenemy.

BATZARRO
Batzarro is the world's worst detective, and the Dark Knight's total opposite.

ARCHENEMIES

LEX LUTHOR'S FOOLPROOF PLAN TO RID THE WORLD OF...

SUPERMAN

- Steal Kryptonite from Batman's secret stash.
- Wrap stolen Kryptonite in a pretty package.
- Add a nice bow.
- Give the "present" to Superman.
- Stand back and laugh out loud as the Kryptonite destroys the Man of Steel forever!

BRICK-SIZED FACT

They may be enemies, but Lex Luthor's minifigure shares his head with Bruce Wayne!

STAT SCAN

NAME:	Alexander Joseph Luthor
FRIENDS:	Darkseid, the Joker
FOES:	Superman, Batman
LIKES:	Power
DISLIKES:	Jokes about being bald

THE RIDDLER

DARKSEID

LEX LUTHOR

BRAINIAC

THE JOKER

0%   100%

CRAZY LAUGH-O-METER

WHERE WOULD SUPER HEROES be without super-villains? Well, they'd probably be taking part in Justice League game nights or relaxing by the pool. Check out the criminals who clash with our champions time and time again.

JUSTICE LEAGUE ARCHENEMIES

1 LEX VS. SUPERMAN
Power-mad Lex dislikes having to look up to anyone. No wonder he wants to destroy a man who can fly.

2 THE JOKER VS. BATMAN
The Joker is Batman's nemesis and opposite. Batman wants law and order, while the Joker loves chaos.

3 CAPTAIN BOOMERANG VS. THE FLASH
The Flash tops the Captain's hit list because he is the only man fast enough to block a speeding boomerang.

4 BLACK MANTA VS. AQUAMAN
Black Manta loathes the sea and everything in it—including Aquaman. He won't rest until the ruler of Atlantis is defeated.

INFO BLAST

BLASTED BOOMERANGS
George "Digger" Harkness, a.k.a. Captain Boomerang, is a crafty crook from Australia. He has an array of specialized boomerangs, which he uses to try to stop The Flash. Luckily, the speedy Super Hero is able to dodge them with ease!

UNIVERSE IN UNITS

1

Luckily for Aquaman, Black Manta appears in just one set so far: Black Manta Deep Sea Strike (76027).

HENCHMEN

EVERY SUPER-VILLAIN worth their salt has henchmen ready to do their dirty work. They may not be the cleverest in the bunch, but henchmen are loyal and brave—except for when they're traitorous and cowardly, of course.

UNIVERSE IN NUMBERS

8

The number of evil LEGO® henchmen (so far!)

STAT SCAN

NAME:	LexCorp Henchman
REAL NAME:	Unknown. Lex always just calls him "you!"
FRIENDS:	Mr. Luthor is his boss, not his friend
FOES:	Superman, Batman
LIKES:	Stealing Kryptonite
DISLIKES:	Having to cancel his coffee break to fight Super Heroes

SIMPLE SIDEKICKS
In the early days, henchmen looked very much alike with their uniform of shady sunglasses, beanie hats, and plain sweaters.

THE JOKER'S GOONS
In 2012, the Joker's henchmen upgraded to lime-green and purple outfits, and freaky face paint. There's no mistaking who these goons work for!

LEX'S UNDERLINGS
With crisp green uniforms, LexCorp ID cards, and goatee beards, Lex Luthor's men look very different to the first henchmen.

THE CHANGING STYLE OF HENCHMEN

ROBO-GOON

The Joker toyed with the idea of employing high-tech clownbots as henchmen. Unfortunately, the robots kept blowing themselves up to get a laugh!

DOs AND DON'Ts
FOR...

HAVING HENCHMEN

DO...

- Invest in black beanie hats. It's what every henchman is wearing this season.

- Keep your henchmen supplied with the latest weaponry, whether that's lasers, laughing-gas canisters, or exploding jack-in-the-boxes.

- Train them to tie good knots— it comes in handy for tying up guards.

DON'T...

- Get too attached to your minions. They're bound to be caught by a Super Hero soon.

- Feed your henchmen toxic popsicles by accident (unless you really want to).

- Be subtle. Splash your face over the back of your goons' jackets!

TOP 3
REASONS TO HAVE HENCHMEN

1 THEY CAN DO CHORES FOR YOU

Why lug dynamite around when you can have a goon do it instead?

2 THEY'RE GETAWAY DRIVERS

Unless they illegally park your car or tank and it gets towed away...

3 THEY CAN TAKE THE RAP

About to get caught by the cops? Then betray your hardworking goons. They deserve to be in prison, not you!

THINK IT'S EASY choosing a side? Think again! Two-Face decides to be a villain on the flick of a coin, while mixed-up Bizarro can't even get being bad right!

INFO BLAST

IN TWO MINDS

It's no wonder Two-Face has trouble deciding whether to be good or evil. He has a split personality as the calm former District Attorney Harvey Dent and also the dangerous criminal Two-Face. He never makes a decision without the flip of a coin!

STAT SCAN

NAME:	Two-Face
REAL NAME:	Harvey Dent
FRIENDS:	The Joker, the Riddler
FOES:	Batman and Robin
LIKES:	Playing heads or tails
DISLIKES:	Matching socks

BRICK-SIZED FACT

The 2006 Two-Face minifigure was the first ever minifigure to have multi-colored printing on its hair piece.

THE CHANGING STYLE OF TWO-FACE

SPLIT SUIT

Two-Face first appeared as a minifigure in 2006, with a black-and-white suit to match the good and bad sides of his personality.

CRAZY COLOR

The divided devil looked slightly happier in 2012 when he added color to his costume to stage a daring robbery at Gotham City Bank.

UNIVERSE IN UNITS

2

The number that Two-Face bases all his crimes around, such as robbing buildings with a "2" in their address.

SIDES

STAT SCAN

NAME:	Bizarro
REAL NAME:	Bizarro No.1
FRIENDS:	Superman
FOES:	Superman
LIKES:	Being bad
DISLIKES:	Being good

AWESOME!

Unlike the effect it has on Superman, green Kryptonite actually makes Bizarro stronger!

SUPERMAN IN REVERSE

Bizarro was created when Lex Luthor used his duplicator ray on the Man of Steel. At first, Superman feared that his terrifying twin was evil, but it soon became clear that Bizarro has a warm heart beneath his odd exterior.

INFO BLAST

BATZARRO

Bizarro was lonely on his home planet Bizarro World, so he used Lex's duplicator ray to create a double of Batman. Batzarro turned out to be the world's worst detective—he can't even put his Utility Belt on the right way up!

HOW TO SPEAK LIKE

BIZARRO

GOOD = BAD

FRIEND = ENEMY

BEAUTY = UGLINESS

SMART = STUPID

LOVE = HATE

STRANGE

Superman's X-ray vision can't see through lead, but Bizarro's X-ray vision can *only* see through lead!

COLD AS ICE
Due to his dangerously low body temperature, Mr. Freeze has to wear cooling armor to survive. Driven crazy by the cold, he wants to plunge the world into eternal winter.

MR. FREEZE'S
CHILLING CATCHPHRASES

"No one is sending me to the cooler!"

"You're out in the cold!"

"Everyone, chill!"

"I'll give anyone the cold shoulder!"

PUT ON ICE
Fed up of the Justice League always foiling his crimes, Mr. Freeze decided to freeze Aquaman in a block of ice, in Arctic Batman vs. Mr. Freeze: Aquaman on Ice (set 76000). Luckily, Batman came to the rescue, blasting the block of ice and freeing Aquaman.

STAT SCAN

NAME:	Mr. Freeze
REAL NAME:	Dr. Victor Fries
FRIENDS:	Poison Ivy, the Joker
FOES:	Batman and Robin
LIKES:	Cold snaps
DISLIKES:	Warm weather

BRICK-SIZED FACT
The space visor piece was made in light blue especially for Mr. Freeze's minifigure.

UNIVERSE IN UNITS
60+
The number of LEGO sets to feature the Penguin's top hat.

CHILLING CRIMINALS

WOW!

Captain Cold's Devastating Ice Shooter is capable of trapping any target in a block of ice—even The Flash!

SOME VILLAINS HARNESS the power of subzero temperatures to carry out their evil deeds. Meet some of the most coldhearted crooks around.

INFO BLAST

Press the ice-cream cone to fire the missile

ICE SCREAM ANYONE?
Even the Joker has been known to add an icy twist to some of his crimes. His cruelest trick yet is selling ice cream laced with laughing potion, in The Tumbler: Joker's Ice Cream Surprise (set 7888). Watch out for the hidden missile in the back of the truck, too!

STAT SCAN

NAME:	Captain Cold
REAL NAME:	Leonard Snart
FRIENDS:	The Trickster, Gorilla Grodd
FOES:	The Flash
LIKES:	Having an ice time
DISLIKES:	Getting confused with Mr. Freeze

COOL CRIMINAL
Oswald Cobblepot, a.k.a. the Penguin, looked every bit the gentleman gangster in his 2006 outfit, complete with top hat, monocle, and snappy suit.

PINSTRIPED PENGUIN
In 2013, the Penguin sported a pinstriped vest and white shirt. He kept his top hat—it gives him extra height to compensate for his short legs!

LUXURY STYLE
He may model himself on a bird from the Antarctic, but this is one Penguin who feels the cold. Luckily for him, in 2014 he gained this fashionable coat.

THE CHANGING STYLE OF THE PENGUIN

FROM ANOTHER PLANET

JUST WHEN YOU THOUGHT Earth's home-grown horrors were bad enough, aliens stand ready to attack from outer space! These extraterrestrials mean extra trouble for the Justice League.

DOs AND DON'TS FOR...

PLANET APOKOLIPS

DO...

- Avoid Darkseid's palace in the capital city of Armaghetto.
- Travel by Boom Tube—interdimensional gateways that zap you from one place to another.

DON'T...

- Take a hot bath in the flaming fire pits that power the planet.
- Say anything bad about Darkseid. His hideous parademon troopers will hunt you down!

STAT SCAN

NAME:	Darkseid
REAL NAME:	Uxas
FRIENDS:	Brainiac
FOES:	The Justice League
LIKES:	Ruling Apokolips with a rod of iron
DISLIKES:	Free will

TREMBLE BEFORE THE POWER OF DARKSEID!

INFO BLAST

HOVER DESTROYER

Darkseid's flying weapon platform enables him to take to the skies to attack Metropolis in Darkseid Invasion (set 76028). The hover platform fires glowing red cannonballs of destructive Omega energy at any meddling Super Heroes.

NO WAY!

Darkseid's name is actually pronounced Dark Side (although Cyborg prefers to call him Dork Side!)

UNIVERSE IN UNITS
245,000

Darkseid's age—he doesn't look a day over 230,000!

STAT SCAN

NAME:	Sinestro
REAL NAME:	Thaal Sinestro
FRIENDS:	None. He hates everybody!
FOES:	Green Lantern
LIKES:	Destroying entire solar systems
DISLIKES:	Being told what to do

INFO BLAST

FALLEN GUARDIAN

Born on the planet Korugar, Sinestro was once the greatest Green Lantern of all. The power went to his head, and Sinestro was banished to an antimatter universe for all time. He escaped, vowing to bring down the Green Lantern Corps.

STRANGE

Sinestro's yellow power ring is powered by fear itself! No wonder the purple menace wants to spread fear across the universe.

INFO BLAST

STOP CALLING ME JOKER! IT'S NOT FUNNY!

MISCHIEF MAKER

The Trickster is happiest when performing pranks with his bag of terrible tricks, which include exploding gum and itching powder. But mistake the pesky prankster for his archrival, the Joker, and that smile quickly disappears from his face!

STAT SCAN

NAME:	The Joker
REAL NAME:	Unknown
FRIENDS:	Harley Quinn, the Penguin
FOES:	Batman and Robin
LIKES:	Having a laugh
DISLIKES:	Taking life seriously

BRICK-SIZED FACT

The Joker has a variety of wacky weapons, but he most frequently appears with his joke "BANG!" gun. The latest version has featured in three sets so far.

BANG!

THE JOKER

THE CHANGING STYLE OF...

FIRST APPEARANCE
The Joker arrived in style in 2006, with a hairstyle that had previously been sported by vampire minifigures, in black.

SLICK MAKEOVER
The manic minifigure got an updated look in 2012 with new hair, a lime-green patterned vest, and an even wider grin!

FANCY FEDORA
In 2014, the Joker swapped hair for a purple hat, which is exclusive to one set—Batman: The Joker Steam Roller (set 76013).

LIGHTS, CAMERAS...
The ultra-creepy clown prince from the Dark Knight movies made his minifigure debut in 2014 in The Tumbler (set 76023).

PRETTY IN PINK
The comic criminal from the 1960s TV show appeared in 2016, complete with a menacing mustache.

WHAT A LAUGH!

LAUGH AND THE CRIMINAL WORLD laughs with you—that's what these bonkers bad guys think anyway! From the Joker's silly schemes to the Riddler's crazy conundrums, these gigglesome gangsters crack as many smiles as they do safes!

The number of superpowers the Trickster possesses—he uses sinister gadgets for his tricks instead!

CATCHPHRASES
THE RIDDLER'S FAVORITE RIDDLES

"The more you take away, the larger it grows. What is it?"
A hole!

"Which president wears the largest hat?"
The one with the biggest head!

"What room can nobody enter?"
A mushroom!

"What kind of machine has ears?"
A train—it has engineers!

INFO BLAST

STAT SCAN

NAME:	The Riddler
REAL NAME:	Edward Nigma
FRIENDS:	The Joker, Catwoman
FOES:	Batman and Robin
LIKES:	Trick questions
DISLIKES:	Not being taken seriously

RIDDLE-ME-THIS
The biggest mystery about the Riddler is why he leaves cryptic clues about his crimes for Batman to solve. No wonder he's always getting caught. He's off to Arkham Asylum (set 7785)—again!

SECRETS OF ARKHAM

BATMAN AND ROBIN keep Arkham Asylum in business, forever delivering dangerous foes to be locked up. Unfortunately, the bad guys and gals of Arkham soon escape, ready to cause fresh chaos in Gotham City!

CRAZY TOWN

Located on the outskirts of Gotham City, Arkham Asylum supposedly keeps the super-villains under lock and key. Sadly, the reality is quite different. Not a day goes by without an escape bid. In fact, some bad guys treat the Asylum as a vacation home, to take a rest until their next breakout!

Q&A — WHY IS THE JOKER SO HAPPY TO BE SENT TO ARKHAM ASYLUM?

Curiously, the Joker always has a smile on his face, even when he's been captured by the Caped Crusader and packed off to Arkham Asylum.

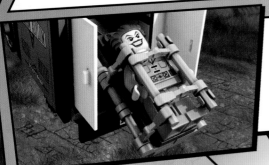

The Joker has been sent to visit Dr. Harleen Quinzel to cure him of his villainous ways. The treatment seems to be going well... But does the Clown Prince of Crime have a plan up his sleeve?

Of course he does! The doctor is really the Joker's accomplice Harley Quinn in disguise! A quick change of costume and she helps him slip out when no one's looking!

VILLAINS IN NUMBERS

1,619 bricks
In Batman: Arkham Asylum Breakout (set 10937)

8 minifigures
Featured in Arkham Asylum Breakout, including the first ever Dr. Harleen Quinzel minifigure

2 sets
Of Arkham Asylum have been released (so far!)

THE MASTER OF FEAR

As a doctor at Arkham, Jonathan Crane studied the fears of its inmates. After discovering a gas that could bring these fears to life, Crane went on a rampage as the sinister Scarecrow. Soon he was back in Arkham—but this time he was behind bars!

CUSTOMIZED CELL

The cells in Arkham have been specially designed for the Asylum's "guests." Poison Ivy's glass chamber stops her from releasing mind-controlling plants into the hospital's corridors.

STAT SCAN

NAME:	Scarecrow
REAL NAME:	Dr. Jonathan Crane
FRIENDS:	The Joker, Harley Quinn
FOES:	Batman and Robin, Blue Beetle
LIKES:	Scaring people
DISLIKES:	Bats—he's scared of them!

UNIVERSE IN UNITS

1921

The year Arkham Asylum first opened its doors.

"IT'S TIME TO
GO GREEN!"

BEST FIENDS

Poison Ivy loves plants so much that she decided to wipe out their biggest threat—humans! The only human Poison Ivy likes is Harley Quinn, who she met at Arkham Asylum. Now, the pair choose their side depending on what they can get out of it.

STAT SCAN

NAME:	Poison Ivy
REAL NAME:	Pamela Isley
FRIENDS:	Harley Quinn, her plants
FOES:	Batman and Robin
LIKES:	Spending time in the greenhouse
DISLIKES:	Anyone being environmentally unfriendly—hero or villain!

THE CHANGING STYLE OF ... HARLEY QUINN

CLOWNING AROUND
In her 2012 outfit, Harley Quinn showed her loyalty to the Joker with her red-and-black clown outfit and jester's hat.

DOCTOR OF DISGUISE
Dr. Harleen Quinzel looks like a respectable doctor in her smart 2013 outfit—but her clown costume is visible under her lab coat!

COSTUME CHANGE
Harley gained a different outfit in 2015, with shorter pants and sleeves, and a necklace made of a string of bells.

NEW STYLE
Harley ditched her jester's hat in 2016 after leaving the Joker. Now, she teams up with whoever she wants—even Batman!

WHEN IS A VILLAIN not a villain? When they turn their terrible talents to solving crimes! These fiendish friends aren't wicked all the time. Harley Quinn, Catwoman, and Poison Ivy have all turned good on occasion... when it suits them!

BRICK-SIZED FACT

Harley and Ivy have appeared in two sets together, Batman: Arkham Asylum Breakout (set 10937) and Jokerland (set 76035).

STRANGE

Poison Ivy briefly teamed up with Batman to stop the Scarecrow using his fear gas on Gotham City. She knew the gas would harm her plants!

THE PURRRFECT PAIR?

Selina Kyle and Bruce Wayne don't always fight like cats and bats. Despite Catwoman being Gotham City's most notorious cat burglar, the two often team up to fight crime. They make a great team, but fickle Catwoman only works with Batman when it suits her.

UNIVERSE IN UNITS

10

The number of different plants that appear in LEGO sets with Poison Ivy.

HARLEY QUINN

CATWOMAN

POISON IVY

0%

100%

VILLAIN-O-METER

WICKED WARSUITS AND ARMOR

VILLAINS LIKE LEX LUTHOR often choose to suit up in order to battle the likes of Superman or Wonder Woman. However, for alien visitors such as General Zod and Faora, wearing armor is a matter of survival!

AWESOME!

Lex Luthor's warsuit is able to withstand a punch from the Man of Steel!

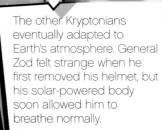

INFO BLAST

LEX-MECH

Lex Luthor breaks out the big guns with his giant power armor (from set 6862). Powered by Kryptonite, this mean green war machine has huge hands ready to put the squeeze on any Super Heroes and a cannon that can blast Superman with Kryptonite radiation.

Q&A

WHY DO KRYPTONIANS NEED TO WEAR SPECIAL ARMOR?

Earth's atmosphere is very different to Krypton, so Kryptonians like Faora and General Zod had to wear armor to breathe when they first arrived.

Superman doesn't need armor as he's been exposed to Earth's atmosphere since he was a baby. His body has naturally adapted to breathe Earth's air.

The other Kryptonians eventually adapted to Earth's atmosphere. General Zod felt strange when he first removed his helmet, but his solar-powered body soon allowed him to breathe normally.

BRICK-SIZED FACT

Superman vs. Power Armor Lex (set 6862) was the first LEGO set to feature Superman, Lex Luthor, and Wonder Woman minifigures.

POWER UP

Lex also has a smaller green-and-purple armor suit (from set 30164). He wears it when wielding his deconstructor gun. The weapon can destroy shiny black objects—like Batman's black vault full of Kryptonite!

Faora's Kryptonian body armor and helmet

UNIVERSE IN UNITS

$60,000,000

The cost of building one of Lex's warsuits. Good thing he's a billionaire!

STAT SCAN

NAME:	Faora
REAL NAME:	Faora-Ul
FRIENDS:	General Zod, Tor-an
FOES:	Superman, Supergirl
LIKES:	War
DISLIKES:	Having to wear armor

ARMED AND DANGEROUS

READY, AIM, FIRE

Don't tell Green Arrow, but Deadshot is the world's greatest marksman. He can hit any target using any weapon—even if it's a huge bazooka! In Gotham City Cycle Chase (set 76053), he wields his stud-shooting bazooka to battle Batman.

WATCH YOUR BACK when the bad guys are in town! The Joker and his pals have huge collections of eye-watering weapons, from laughing gas and remote-controlled penguins to sharp swords and scorpions.

Stud-shooting bazooka

INFO BLAST

LAZARUS PIT

The secret headquarters of the League of Assassins holds a magical Lazarus Pit (from set 76056). No matter what injuries villains suffer in battle, Rā's al Ghūl's magical pit can restore them to health!

DEATHSTROKE

Thanks to a secret military experiment, Deathstroke became the ultimate super-soldier. The agile warrior uses a variety of weapons, including this powerful sword.

RA'S AL GHUL

The founder of the League of Assassins is a master of hand-to-hand combat. He is hundreds of years old, so he has had plenty of time to practice!

TALIA AL GHUL

Like father like daughter—Talia al Ghūl takes after her dad with her sword skills. She always makes sure her sabres are sharp.

WEAPON WARRIORS

NAME:	Deadshot
REAL NAME:	Floyd Lawton
FRIENDS:	Harley Quinn, Katana
FOES:	Batman and Robin
LIKES:	Hitting the target
DISLIKES:	Wasting ammunition

BRICK-SIZED FACT

Rā's al Ghūl's black scorpion is also found in 43 other doom-laden sets!

Jetpack allows Deadshot to blast Super Heroes from up high

28-01 11090

TOP 6
WICKED WEAPONS

1 ROBO-PENGUINS

Who but the Penguin would employ remote-controlled Penguins? The tiny drones waddle into dangerous situations to wreak more havoc!

2 LAUGHING GAS MISSILES

The Joker's favorite chemical concoction makes you get the giggles... while he gets away with your family jewels!

3 FEAR-GAS GRENADES

Just one sniff of the Scarecrow's fear gas will plunge you into a living nightmare. Your greatest fears come to life in front of your eyes!

4 UMBRELLA

The Penguin's collection of umbrellas hides a multitude of booby traps, from blades to knock-out gas!

5 CRACKLING CREAM PIE

The Joker's tasty-looking weapon contains the Clown Prince of Crime's own secret ingredient—crackling electricity. What a shock!

6 SCORPION

Not only do the League of Assassins keep their swords sharp, they also send scorpions scuttling into the homes of their enemies.

UNIVERSE IN UNITS
90+

Deathstroke's sword has appeared in more than 90 LEGO sets, in six different colors.

SCARY SKILLS

STAT SCAN

NAME:	Killer Moth
REAL NAME:	Drury Walker
FRIENDS:	Anyone who pays him
FOES:	Batman and Robin
LIKES:	Bright lights
DISLIKES:	Mothballs

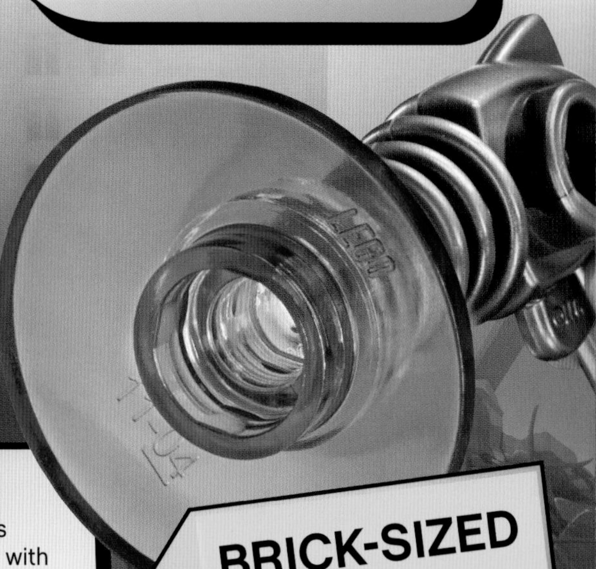

MANY SO-CALLED super-villains actually have no superpowers at all. Instead, they have developed sinister skills. Some, like Killer Moth and Deathstroke, have learned martial arts. Other crooks, such as the Joker and Harley Quinn, rely on their evil brains to get ahead.

INFO BLAST

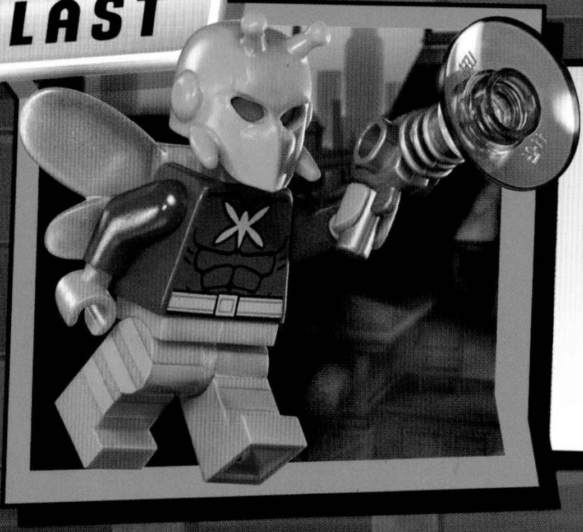

THE ANTI-BATMAN

Like Batman, Killer Moth makes up for his lack of superpowers with his martial arts skills and high-tech equipment. He mimicks everything about Batman—he has a Mothcave, a Mothmobile, and a Moth-Signal! But where Batman helps the police, Killer Moth helps Gotham's wickedest villains.

BRICK-SIZED FACT

Killer Moth's wings appear in other LEGO sets as fairy wings. They were made in neon orange especially for him.

CROOKED CHEMISTRY

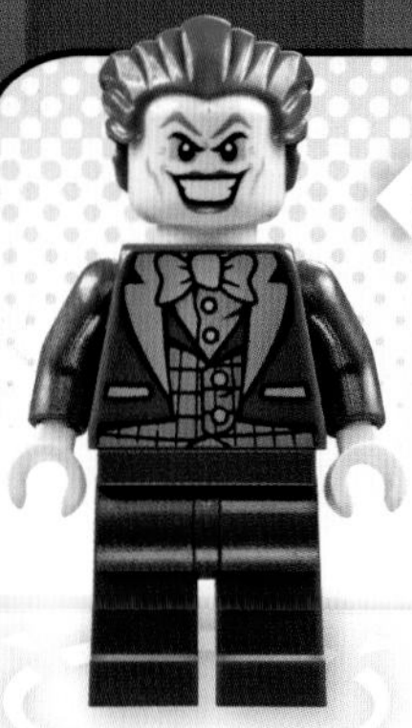

JOKER

The Joker is a chemical genius, able to whip up wicked potions at the drop of a hat. His laughing gas makes anyone think he's a hoot even when he's robbing them!

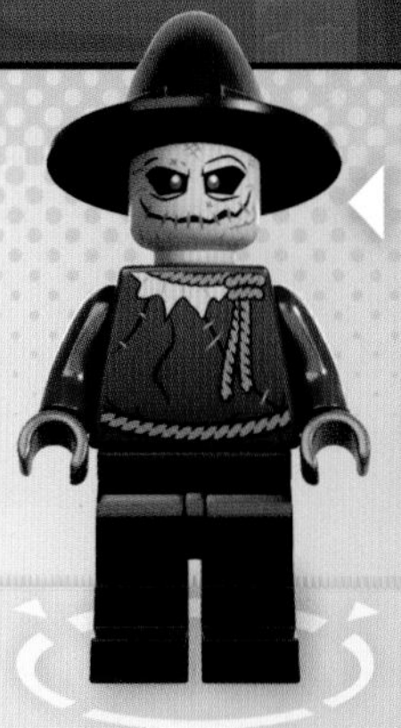

SCARECROW

While the Joker's gas makes people laugh, the Scarecrow's homemade fear gas does the opposite. It makes his victims see their fears, leaving them shaking in their boots!

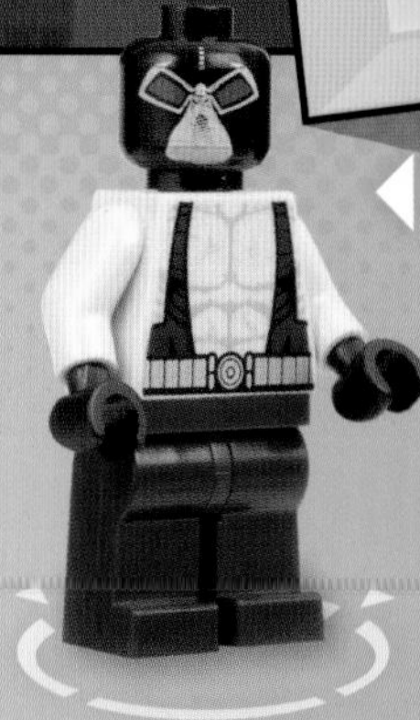

BANE

Bane only uses his chemical concoction, which he has named Venom, on himself. He is naturally small, but the bubbling yellow mixture transforms him into a muscular menace.

UNIVERSE IN UNITS
234026

Killer Moth's prison number. It was while he was in prison that he decided to become the "anti-Batman."

TECH HARLEY'S TRUCK

"I AM THE BEST AT EVERYTHING I DO!"

MERCENARY IN TRAINING

Assassin Deathstroke was taught everything he knows by martial-arts expert, Madame Mantis. He trained alongside her top student—the young Bruce Wayne! He had no idea that Bruce would go on to become one of his greatest foes, Batman.

GETAWAY DRIVER

Harley Quinn is a skilled driver. She is happiest when behind the wheel of a crazy car, like her Hammer Truck (from set 7886). Her speedy getaways make her the driver of choice in any criminal caper. Watch out, though—she laughs at the idea of traffic laws!

DANGER IN THE DEPTHS

FORGET SEA MONSTERS! The scariest things beneath the waves are aquatic super-villains. Black Manta tops the chart of criminals you don't want to meet on a scuba dive, but the Penguin is close behind—thanks to his sinister seabird submersible.

INFO BLAST

Flick missiles

ROBOSHARK ATTACK

When Black Manta captured Robin in Black Manta Deep Sea Strike (set 76027), he left this remote-controlled RoboShark to guard his hostage. Robin didn't know what was scarier—its sharp teeth or its laser missiles!

Black Manta's insignia

STAT SCAN

NAME:	Black Manta
FRIENDS:	None
FOES:	Aquaman, Batman, Robin
LIKES:	Not a lot
DISLIKES:	Atlantis

AWESOME!

Black Manta's bizarre-looking helmet fires lasers from its bug-like eyes!

BRICK-SIZED FACT

The translucent red cockpit piece on Black Manta's Sea Saucer is only available in one set: Black Manta Deep Sea Strike (set 76027).

Spinning rear propeller

POWERS

BLACK MANTA

Black Manta doesn't have any superpowers, but he has trained his body to peak physical condition. Now, he can swim through the sea as fast as a torpedo.

VILLAINOUS VESSELS

SEA SAUCER

Black Manta's Sea Saucer (from set 76027) casts a dark shadow over the seabed. Its hull can become a powerful bio-magnet that causes any living thing to stick to its side, including Aquaman!

DUCK BOAT

No, you're not quacking up—that really is a boat shaped like a rubber duck. The Penguin's dinghy (from set 76010) may look silly, but it has plenty of firepower, with flick missiles under each wing.

THE U99 SUBMARINE

The Penguin's Submarine (from set 7885) is bristling with torpedoes and even has a tally of the times he's fought Batman etched into its side.

KILLER CROC'S SPEED BOAT

This toothy speedboat (from set 7780) is fast enough to chase even the Batboat. Armed with swamp missiles, the small craft packs a punch, but it is a snug fit for Killer Croc.

BATTLE CHOMPER

With his newly beefed-up body, Croc needs a bigger boat. With its mechanical jaws, the Battle Chomper (from set 76055) has plenty of bite. Captain Boomerang rides along in the look-out tower.

UNIVERSE IN UNITS

16

Number of teeth on Killer Croc's Battle Chomper.

GO WILD

It's a jungle out there! These beastly bad guys fight tooth and claw to take over the world. You'd have to be animal crackers to stand in their way.

STAT SCAN

NAME:	Gorilla Grodd
FRIENDS:	Captain Cold, the Trickster
FOES:	The Flash
LIKES:	Bananas
DISLIKES:	Monkeying around

TREMBLE BEFORE GRODD!

Mind control equipment

UNIVERSE IN UNITS

600

Gorilla Grodd's sizeable weight in pounds (270 in kilograms).

TOP 5
FACTS ABOUT GORILLA GRODD

1 Grodd is the king of Gorilla City, located deep in the heart of Africa.

2 He gained his extreme intelligence when a radioactive meteor struck his jungle home.

3 He later developed the awesome power of mind control, which allows him to control other people's thoughts.

4 This angry ape hates humans. He even went back in time to try to wipe humans from history!

5 Grodd's love of bananas has caused him to slip up and get caught by the good guys time and time again!

KILLER CROC

INFO BLAST

DRIVEN BATTY

Medical man Dr. Kirk Langstrom got more than he bargained for when he concocted a cure for his hearing loss. The special serum transformed him into the hideous flying bat-like monster known as Man-Bat!

MINI CROC

In 2006, the revolting reptile made his one and only splash as a minifigure in Gotham City's underworld. Batman soon wiped that toothy grin from Killer Croc's scaly face.

SUPERSIZED CROC

You can't keep a bad croc down! The vicious villain scaled up in 2016 to bully Gotham City with his muscly new build. What he lacks in brains, he more than makes up for in size!

BRICK-SIZED FACT

Killer Croc's bumpy head mold is unique to his minifigure, although he does share his body mold with Gorilla Grodd.

STRANGE

Grodd can make a monkey out of anyone by transferring his own mind into someone else's body!

KILLER CROC

GORILLA GRODD

GENIUS-O-METER

0%   100%

STAT SCAN

NAME:	Killer Croc
REAL NAME:	Waylon Jones
FRIENDS:	Captain Bomerang, the Penguin
FOES:	Batman and Robin
LIKES:	Getting a bite to eat
DISLIKES:	Handbags and shoes

EVIL IN THE SKIES

CITIZENS OF EARTH must keep a vigilant eye on the skies—super-villains sometimes attack from above! These bad guys have the best aircraft stolen money can buy.

STRANGE

When he landed on Earth, Zod realized he didn't need to use spaceships anymore because he could now fly like Superman!

Q&A HOW DOES ZOD'S DROPSHIP LAND?

Kryptonian General Zod and his henchmen, Faora and Tor-An, use their Dropship in Superman: Battle of Smallville (set 76003) to try to take over Smallville. When diving through the Earth's atmosphere, the Dropship's fins are kept in their flight formation.

When it is ready to land, the fins swivel around to point down, so that the Dropship can land on them. This means the Dropship's rotating laser cannon remains suspended above the ground at all times.

STEALTH   SPEED   STYLE

VEHICLE VITALS

Tor-An mans the Dropship

BRICK-SIZED FACT

Lex Luthor's LexCorp helicopter (from set 76046) is equipped with eight flick missiles.

The Dropship has hidden compartments to store Zod's stash of Kryptonian guns

UNIVERSE IN UNITS 12

The number of LEGO DC Comics Super Heroes sets to include aircraft.

AWFUL AIRCRAFT

THE JOKER'S HELICOPTER

There's no mistaking who owns this fiendish helicopter (from set 7782). It is decorated with the Joker's face for all to see.

THE JOKER'S SECOND HELICOPTER

The Clown Prince of Crime's upgraded chopper (from set 6863) includes bigger laughing-gas bombs and four flick missiles.

THE SCARECROW'S BIPLANE

This propellered flier (from set 7786) looks a little old-fashioned, but it's the perfect way for the Scarecrow to spread his fear gas.

LEXCORP HELICOPTER

This chopper (from set 76046) is loaded with Kryptonite missiles. No wonder Lois risks everything to photograph the evidence!

STAT SCAN

NAME:	General Zod
REAL NAME:	Dru-Zod
FRIENDS:	Foara, Tor-an
FOES:	Jor-El, Superman
LIKES:	War
DISLIKES:	The Phantom Zone

DANGER ON THE ROAD

This fleet of villainous vehicles do more than break traffic laws—they break everything on the road, too! It's a demolition derby every day in Gotham City. No wonder Batman needs so many cars to give chase!

VILLAINS IN NUMBERS

$325,000
The approximate cost of building a life-size LEGO Tumbler

500 horsepower
The power of the Tumbler's engine

160 mph
(260 km/h) The Tumbler's top speed

BRICK-SIZED FACT

The Tumbler's rear tires feature in around 60 LEGO sets, including racing cars and ice-cream trucks.

TUMBLER TERROR
Having Bane on the loose in Gotham City is bad enough. But the news that the masked menace has stolen Wayne Enterprise's experimental all-terrain vehicles (from set 76001) is simply terrifying.

Flick missiles fire from hidden missile launcher

Roof flips up to allow Bane to enter the tumbler

SPEED STEALTH STYLE

VEHICLE VITALS

SPEED DEMONS

THE JOKER'S STEAM ROLLER

No bank clerk can stop the Joker steaming in to make a withdrawal in this riotous roller (from set 76013). Walls are demolished and roadblocks are flattened in its path.

THE RIDDLER'S DRAGSTER

The quickest getaway car ever constructed, the Riddler's dragster (from set 76012) can reach speeds of over 280mph (450 kph). It also comes with swag bags to store stolen cash.

HARLEY'S HAMMER TRUCK

Watch out! Harley's traffic-trashing truck with huge hammer (from set 7886) is ready to hit the road and anything on it. Harley's even scrawled "Whack-a-Bat" on the malicious mallet!

TWO-FACE'S CAR

Why bother cracking a safe when you can just steal the entire thing? Two-Face's terrifying truck (from set 6864) has seen a lot of action, judging by the many bullet holes in its paintwork.

THE DRILL TANK

There's a mole in the Batcave! Bane once burrowed beneath the ground in this deadly drill-dozer (from set 6860) to break into Batman's subterranean lair.

AWESOME!

With its engine purring, Catwoman's Catcyle (from set 6858) can speed away from the scene of any crime. It always lands on its wheels when forced to make a sudden jump.

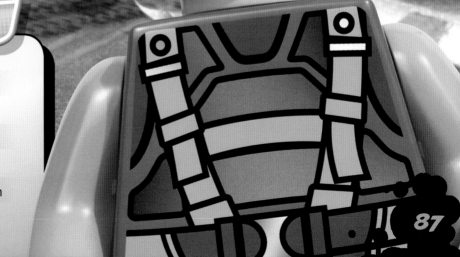

STAT SCAN

NAME:	Bane
REAL NAME:	Unknown
FRIENDS:	None whatsover
FOES:	Batman
LIKES:	Causing mayhem
DISLIKES:	Law and order

SPOT THE DIFFERENCE

To complete his task of cataloging the universe, Brainiac has created an army of robotic duplicates of himself. They can always tell each other apart—even though they all look exactly the same!

BRAINIAC 1.1
The most advanced robot in the universe.

BRAINIAC 1.2
Wants to destroy Brainiac 1.1 so *he* will be the most advanced robot in the universe.

BRAINIAC 1.3
Longs to be promoted to Brainiac 1.2.

BRAINIAC 1.4
In charge of cleaning Brainiac 1.1's fleet of spaceships.

Q&A WHY WAS BRAINIAC BUILT?

Brainiac was originally designed to be the universe's ultimate artificial intelligence. His mission was to catalog every planet in existence.

However, a malfunction warped his programming. Now he uses a shrink ray to miniaturize entire planets so he can store them in jars!

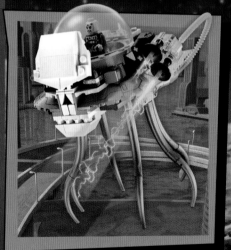

SKULL SHIP
In Brainiac Attack (set 76040), Brainiac used his Skull Ship to invade Metropolis. This tentacled spaceship comes with twin laser cannons. It also fires time-twisting energy beams from its eyes, so Brainiac can zap people back to the Stone Age!

VILLAINS IN NUMBERS

161 bricks
Make up Brainiac's Skull Ship (from set 76040)

121 robot drones
Stand ready for battle inside the Skull Ship

1 yellow staff
Is included in Green Lantern vs. Sinestro (set 76025). Sinestro uses this power staff to guard the stolen Green Lantern

ALIEN TECH

The universe is full of intergalactic villains who come equipped with their own high-tech alien weaponry. Some are even a form of technology themselves, like the hyper-intelligent robot, Brainiac. From sinister shrink rays to tentacled spaceships, alien technology tests Earth's heroes to their limits.

"MY MASTER PLAN CONTINUES TO UNFOLD!"

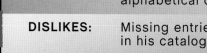

EVIL LAIRS

All super-villains need their own lair. It's essential that they have a place where they can hatch diabolical plots, concoct powerful potions, store their loot, and unwind after battling Super Heroes.

SCORCHING SPEEDS

Former acrobat Robin never got the hang of motorcycle stunts. The poor Boy Wonder is hanging upside down from Harley's bike as it approaches the flames. He needs to find a way to escape before he singes his cape!

HIDEOUS HIDEAWAYS

LEXCORP TOWER

Lex Luthor pretends to be an honest businessman, but really his company, LexCorp, is just a front for his evil schemes. Lex made sure LexCorp's headquarters was just taller than the *Daily Planet* building.

THE HALL OF DOOM

This is the headquarters of the Legion of Doom, which was founded by Lex Luthor to fight the Justice League. Lex transformed the lair into a flying fortress!

BRAINIAC'S SKULL SHIP

Brainiac stores his collection of shrunken planets in his skull-shaped starship. The hyper-intelligent bad guy studies the mini citizens of the tiny planets from his ship.

WHAT A FOWL TRICK

The Penguin's Deadly Duckies ride is no fun at all. The ride is full of dynamite! Beast Boy needs to break free of his handcuffs and escape—being careful not to fall into the shark-infested waters below!

BIZARRO WORLD

Superman tricked Bizarro into setting up home on this crazy cuboid planetoid. Here, everything is reversed—down is up and bad is good. This suited strange Bizarro, and he was soon joined by Batzarro.

NONE OF THE FUN OF THE FAIR

Happy Land was once Gotham City's number-one amusement park. Sadly, those days are gone. The Joker has transformed the happiest place in Gotham City into a horrific hideout, bursting with traps to snare Robin and the other Teen Titans.

TOP 4
THINGS EVERY EVIL LAIR NEEDS

1 A SECRET ENTRANCE

There's no point in having a hidden hideaway if everyone knows how to get in!

2 AN UTTERLY EVIL COMPUTER

Villains need to keep up with technology to compete with high-tech heroes like Batman.

3 A SHARK PIT

Not only do they make great pets, sharks are a convenient way to get rid of former employees.

4 A WEAPONS STORE

This is essential for stashing custard pies, exploding fish, and acid-squirting flowers.

MIRROR IMAGE

Anyone who gets trapped in the Joker's Hall of Mirrors could be lost for hours! Next to the Hall of Mirrors is a toxic pit, which is ideal for disposing of pesky Super Heroes or disobedient henchmen.

HOW BAD ARE YOU?

Congratulations! The super-villains want you to join them in their quest for world domination. But are you wicked enough to join the ranks of the super-villains, or will you be happy to serve as a henchman for the rest of your criminal career? Answer these questions to find out.

You discover a giant lump of Kryptonite. What do you do?

A Grind it up and use it to make special glow-in-the-dark Kryptonite cookies! Then send them to Superman and laugh loudly as the Man of Steel chokes on his radioactive snack.

B Hope someone else tells you what to do with it.

C Contact Green Lantern and ask him to blast the Kryptonite into a faraway sun, so that it can't harm Superman.

There's a cat stuck up a tree. What do you do?

A Invent a despicable Monsterfier Ray and use it to turn the helpless kitty into a fierce three-headed beast (with extra tentacles).

B Carry your boss's despicable Monsterfier Ray to the tree, trying not to drop it.

C Fly up there and rescue the poor kitty. Isn't he cute?

You don't have enough money to buy the latest issue of *The Evil Genius* magazine. What do you do?

A Build a Mole Machine to tunnel into a bank. Steal all the money so that you'll be rich enough to subscribe forever!

B Ask your boss if you can borrow his copy. (Don't forget to say please!)

C It doesn't matter—you'd never read such trash anyway. You prefer *Truth and Justice Monthly*.

Brainiac is attacking Earth with a fleet of 1,958 Skull Ships. What do you do?

A Join forces with the rotten robot. Once Brainiac has conquered Earth, you can double-cross him and take power for yourself.

B Run and hide from the Skull Ships. You've seen some scary things in your time, but these are TERRIFYING!

C Intercept the alien fleet in the Javelin. The odds are stacked against you, but it's your duty to protect Earth.

The Joker has escaped from Arkham Asylum. What do you do?

A Rob Gotham City Museum while Batman and Robin are busy looking for him.

B Put on some clownish face paint and hope he hires you.

C Cancel your dinner plans and pull on your cape and cowl. You won't rest until the Joker is safely back behind bars.

You discover a magical amulet that can send people back through time. What do you do?

A Dispatch the Justice League back to prehistoric times. With any luck, they'll all be eaten by a hungry Tyrannosaurus rex.

B Go back to this morning. You forgot to pick up your boss's coffee, and he's threatening to feed you to his robot penguins.

C Crush it with your bare hands to ensure its power will never be used for evil.

You discover the location of Superman's Fortress of Solitude. What do you do?

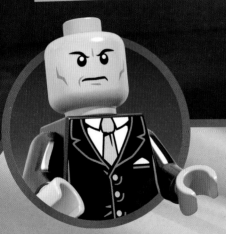

A Break in and steal all of Superman's Kryptonian secrets. No one will be able to stop you from taking over the world now!

B Complain that it's really cold and ask your boss to use Superman's Kryptonian secrets to make you a snowsuit.

C Drop over for pizza. You're sure Superman won't mind! Perhaps after you've watched a movie together you can team up on a heroic mission or two?

Lois Lane is falling to her doom from the top of a tall building! What do you do?

A Take a selfie as she plummets to the ground. After all, you were the one who pushed her!

B Grab a quick sandwich. You haven't had your lunch break yet.

C Save Lois just in the nick of time. Phew! You can't stick around for an interview, though. You need to stop a natural disaster on the other side of the world.

MOSTLY A

Congratulations! You are as mean and villainous as Lex Luthor himself. In fact, he'll probably see you as a threat and blast you with his Destructor Ray. Sorry.

MOSTLY B

You would make a great henchman. Actually, you'd probably be a dreadful henchman, but that's the trouble with goons these days. You just can't get the staff!

MOSTLY C

Your bravery and dedication to justice mean you're poorly suited to life as a super-villain. In fact, you're a member of the Justice League, aren't you?

SET LIST

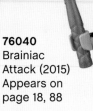

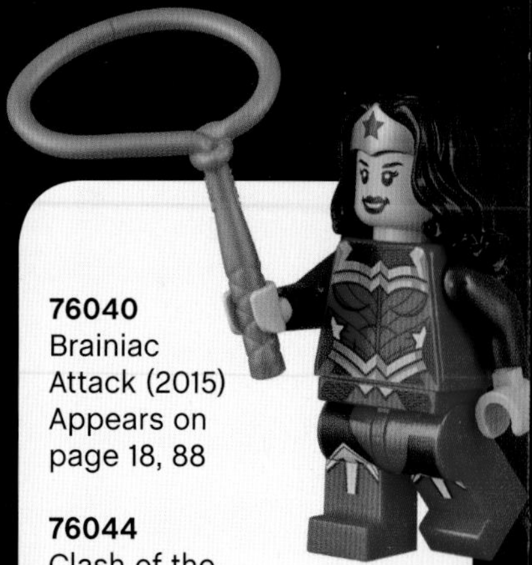

INDEX

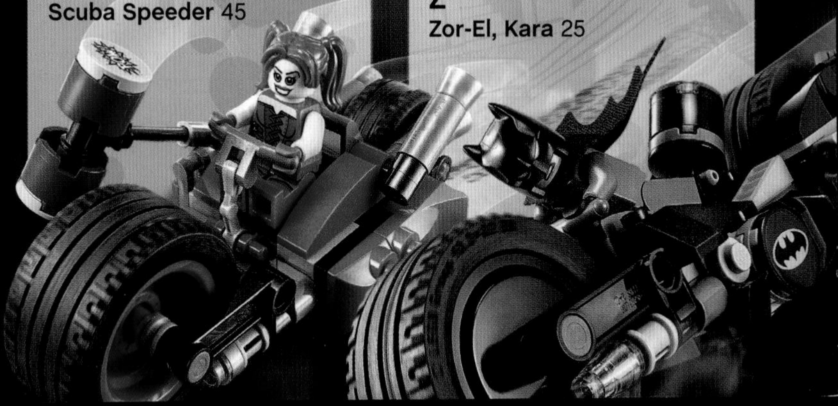

Penguin
Random
House

Senior Editor	Helen Murray
Project Art Editors	Jon Hall and Rhys Thomas
Editor	Rosie Peet
Additional designers	Ian Midson and Stefan Georgiou
Pre-production Producer	Marc Staples
Producer	Louise Daly
Managing Editor	Paula Regan
Managing Art Editor	Jo Connor
Publisher	Julie Ferris
Art Director	Lisa Lanzarini
Publishing Director	Simon Beecroft

Cover design by Rhys Thomas

Dorling Kindersley would like to thank Randi Sorensen, Paul Hansford, Heidi K. Jensen, Martin Leighton Lindhardt and the LEGO DC Super Heroes team at the LEGO Group, Benjamin Harper, Melanie Swartz, and Thomas Zellers at Warner Bros. Consumer Products, Elena Jarmoskaite for design assistance, Alexandra Beeden for proofreading, Helen Peters for writing the index, Markos Chouris for additional photography on page 17, and Gary Ombler for additional photography on pages 18–19.

First American Edition, 2017
Published in the United States by DK Publishing
345 Hudson Street, New York, NY 10014

Page design copyright © 2017
Dorling Kindersley Limited
DK, a Division of Penguin Random House LLC
17 18 19 20 21 10 9 8 7 6 5 4 3
004–298010–May/17

A catalog record for this book is available from the Library of Congress.

ISBN 978-1-4654-6078-3

DK books are available at special discounts when purchased in bulk for sales promotions, premiums, fund-raising, or educational use. For details, contact: DK Publishing Special Markets, 345 Hudson Street, New York, New York 10014
SpecialSales@dk.com

Printed and bound in China

www.lego.com
www.dk.com

A WORLD OF IDEAS:
SEE ALL THERE IS TO KNOW

DORL37231